ON FOOT

IN JOSHUA TREE NATIONAL PARK

A COMPREHENSIVE HIKING GUIDE

PATTY FURBUSH

M.I. ADVENTURE PUBLICATIONS

M.I. Adventure Publications publishes outdoor guides, park guides for families, and park related children's books. Find out more about our books by visiting our website at www.blissnet.com/~miap. You can order books or get information by contacting us at the address below.

First Printing, March 1986
Second Edition, March 1987
Third Edition, February 1992
Fourth Edition, July 1995 — Revised, September 2001
Fifth Edition , January 2005

All photos by the author except as noted

Cover Photo: Hikers near the start of the Boy Scout Trail

ISBN 0-9713571-3-7

CAUTION:
Outdoor recreational activities, including hiking, can be potentially dangerous. The scope of this book does not allow for the presentation of all risks and hazards associated with hiking activities. This guide should not replace your judgment and decision making skills. You are responsible for being prepared for the outdoor activities involved, knowing the potential risks, and taking proper safety precautions.

M.I. Adventure Publications
P.O. Box 277
Moose, WY 83012

(307)739-2385
miap@blissnet.com

To my parents
Lt. Colonel and Mrs. Richard D. Furbush

Acknowledgements

Special thanks to Kip Knapp, Jim Schlinkmann, Colette Bien, Richie Knapp, and Dan Wirth for accompanying me on many hikes. Thanks to Jim Schlinkmann, Peggy Furbush, Lois and Robert Diefendorf, Matthew King, Aleta McCardle, Mary Nutter, Kathleen and Harvey King, Kip Knapp, Todd Swain, Colette Bien, Terry Lee, Gary Garrett, Debbie Brenchley, Bill Truesdell, Joan Jackson, Pat Flanagan, Tim Bertrand, Jeff Ohlfs, Cindy Von Halle, Dar Spearing, Erica Stone, Teresa Griswold, Rosie Pepito, Howard Simpkinson, Elize Van Zandt, Joe Zarki, Ken Hornback, Chuck Nisbet, Jeffrey Black, Richie Knapp, and Ken Love for providing assistance with the research and technical preparation of this book.

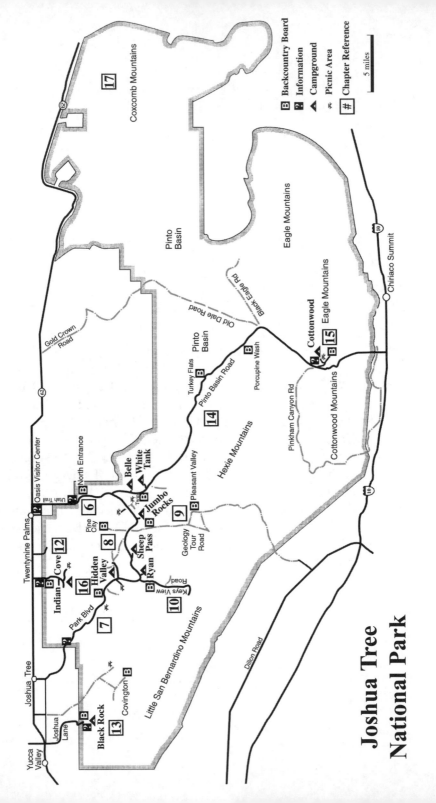

Joshua Tree National Park

Legend:
- B Backcountry Board
- ? Information
- ▲ Campground
- ⚘ Picnic Area
- # Chapter Reference

5 miles

Coxcomb Mountains

17

Pinto Basin

Eagle Mountains

Black Eagle Rd

Old Dale Road

Gold Crown Road

Turkey Flats B
Pinto Basin

14

Porcupine Wash

Cottonwood
B 15

Eagle Mountains

Chiriaco Summit

10

Pinto Basin Road

Hexie Mountains

Pinkham Canyon Rd

Cottonwood Mountains

Oasis Visitor Center
North Entrance
Utah Trail
?

Belle ▲
White Tank ▲

Twin Tanks

Jumbo Rocks ⚘
B
6

B Pleasant Valley

9

Geology Tour Road

Pine City
B
8

Sheep Pass ▲
Ryan B
Keys View Road

Twentynine Palms

12
Indian Cove ▲ ⚘
B 16
Hidden Valley
B ⚘

7

⚘

10

Park Blvd

Little San Bernardino Mountains

Joshua Tree

Joshua Lane

Covington B ⚘

Black Rock ▲ B

13

Yucca Valley

Dillon Road

Table of Contents

Maps and Information Notification

The topographical maps included in this book are based on USGS topographical maps modified and revised by M. I. Adventure Publications. M. I. Adventure Publications is in no way responsible for lost persons, personal injury, damage to property, or violation of the law in connection with the use of the maps and information included in this guide.

8

Editor's Note:

Do you want to be a part of the next edition of
On Foot in Joshua Tree National Park?

In 1994, Congress created Joshua Tree National Park. Previously, the park area was a national monument. Besides changing the park status, Congress added 234,000 acres to the park area. Most of the new acreage is designated wilderness. Very few hikes within the new park area have been documented in writing.

If you plan to explore these new areas, you may be interested in contributing to the next edition of this book. If you discover a notable hike and would like us to consider it for inclusion in the next edition, write to us at: M.I. Adventure Publications, Attention: Next Edition, P.O. Box 277, Moose, WY 83012.

Please include the following information: 1. Type of hike — cross-country or road-trail. 2. Approximate mileage. 3. Estimated time for completion (leisurely). 4. Difficulty — easy, moderate, or strenuous and the technical difficulty. 5. Starting and ending points. 6. Hike summary including the highlights along the hike. 7. Route description including a detailed description of any confusing areas. 8. Map — a copy of a topographical map showing the starting point, hike route, and destination. (Please provide us with the name of the topographical map.) 9. Your name, address, and phone number so we may contact you for clarification and acknowledgement. 10. Any additional comments.

Cautionary Note:

In 2001, the National Park Service began implementing a new Backcountry Management Plan for Joshua Tree National Park. The implementation is still in the beginning stages. As a result of this plan, access roads, trailheads, and trails may be moved or upgraded in the near future. Bear in mind that this may create some inaccuracies in the current hike and access descriptions. Be sure to use good judgment and orienteering skills to augment this guide. Check with the National Park Service for information on recent changes.

Enjoy your explorations!

The Editor

*Joshua Tree National Park is a special place
that delights hikers of all ages.*

Chapter 1
JOSHUA TREE NATIONAL PARK
A SPECIAL PLACE

The pink illumination of dawn cloaks an extensive array of gigantic boulder piles and monolithic rock formations. Rugged mountains cast shadows across an immense basin that stretches mile after seemingly endless mile. As the shadows recede, the rising sun brings forth the color and life of the daylight hours. Delicate white petals of the tidy-tip flower shimmer in the breeze. An antelope ground squirrel scampers past the flower leaving a repeating pattern in the sand. Overhead a high-pitched cry emits from a solitary red-tailed hawk as he circles in the vivid blue skies. Deep within an isolated canyon, the mysterious descending echoes of a canyon wren's song ring forth from beneath a sentinel of palm trees.

The warm sun continues its daily journey across the open skies, and eventually the shadows begin to lengthen. As dusk descends, the pink illumination returns to highlight a high rocky cliff from where a golden eagle takes flight. An owl hoots and two coyotes exchange eerie howls in the approaching darkness. Black forests of still and multiarmed tree-figures create a grand silhouette against a sunset blaze of oranges and reds. A sea of stars begins sparkling throughout the clear night skies. The colorless land now cloaked in darkness beckons forth the life of the nighttime hours....

These are the intricate images of the vast and interwoven wonders of a desert wilderness. It is a wilderness that is among one of this country's national treasures. It is a wilderness whose life, secrets and magic cannot be fully enjoyed and appreciated until it is traveled and explored on foot.

Joshua Tree National Park, located in the heart of southern California, is this wilderness treasure. It is a 1240 square mile hikers' playground. The area attracts multitudes of people who drive the roads to gaze upon desert wonders. However, the backcountry remains quiet, undisturbed, and offers a beautiful, adventuresome retreat for those willing to set out on foot. The Colorado and Mojave Deserts merge within this desert playground creating an opportunity to compare and explore two separate desert ecosystems.

Joshua trees frame giant boulders in the Mojave Desert.

Mojave Desert

The Mojave Desert, which predominates the central and western half of the park, is the higher, wetter, and cooler of the two desert ecosystems. It exists largely at elevations greater than 2000' and hence is commonly called the high desert. The Mojave is home for the large forests of Joshua trees, which grow only at elevations over 3000'. Joshua trees are yucca plants, members of the lily family.

A second beautiful curiosity, which exists within this higher portion of the park, is the unique collection of gigantic boulder formations that tower above the Joshua trees. The mere sight of this geologic oddity makes one wonder what magnificent force rolled the rocks together to create the formations.

The boulder piles actually formed underground. Liquid rock oozed up, cooled, and crystallized beneath the core of existing older rock known as Pinto Gneiss. The younger, igneous rock, known as monzogranite, formed with many irregularly spaced horizontal and vertical cracks. Water filtered down through the Pinto Gneiss into the cracks in the monzogranite. The water caused a chemical reaction that transformed the outer layers of this new rock into clay. Uplifting and erosion of the Pinto Gneiss gradually worked to expose the monzogranite rock to the earth's surface. Once exposed, the soft clay covering the monzogranite eroded away leaving the rock with rounded edges. As the clay eroded from the cracks, the resulting large rounded rocks collapsed into piles creating the boulder formations.

Tall, spindly ocotillos flourish in the Colorado Desert.

RUSSELL SCOFIELD

Colorado Desert

The Colorado Desert, which predominates the southern and eastern half of the park, lies at an elevation generally less than 3000'. This desert has its own characteristic vegetation. Ocotillo and the jumping cholla cactus are among the most notable of the Colorado Desert plants. There are a greater variety and a more abundance of cacti in the Colorado Desert than in the Mojave Desert. There is also a greater variety of trees. Mesquite, palo verdes, and smoke trees flourish along many of the sandy washes.

One feature that cannot go unmentioned when describing the Colorado Desert section of the park is the Pinto Basin. This immense basin, measuring close to 200 square miles, is mostly untouched by road or human foot. Only two roads travel through the basin. Pinto Basin Road travels along the southwestern edge of the basin. Old Dale Road, a dirt road, travels north to south through the center of the basin. The majority of the basin remains a wilderness.

Oases and Mountains

Five oases provide a third type of ecosystem found within the park. The life that centers around these vibrant islands is in contrast to the arid surroundings in which they are found. Water, either on the surface or not far below, nourishes concentrations of lush grasses, native fan palms, cottonwoods and other water-loving plants. The oases provide an important life source and home for many species of plants, birds, and other wildlife.

There are many mountains located throughout the park both in and around the Colorado and Mojave deserts and around the oases. They are the high, rugged, rocky mountains of the Little San Bernardino, Hexie, Pinto, Coxcomb, Eagle and Cottonwood mountain ranges. In the cooler, moister, upper reaches of these mountains is yet a fourth type of habitat. Pinyon pines, junipers, scrub oak, and red-barked manzanita, intermingled with the more commonly associated desert vegetation, provide for beautiful terrain and additional variety for hikers and backpackers.

Wildlife

On foot in the quiet backcountry is the best way to seek and enjoy the desert wildlife. There are about 40 species of reptiles and amphibians and 40 species of mammals that make their home in the park. Some of the more notable mammal species includes desert bighorn sheep and mountain lions.

In addition, over 200 species of birds have been recorded within the park. The National Audubon Society considers Joshua Tree National Park to be one of the best birding areas in Southern California.

Each species of wildlife within the park is an important and inseparable part of the desert ecosystem. The feared rattlesnake and uncomely chuckwalla lizard are as equally important in the desert web of life as the red-tailed hawk, the coyote, and the desert bighorn. Read the pamphlets available from the visitor centers to learn about, identify, and locate the abundance of wildlife.

History

In the early days before the park was established, there was another form of wildlife that made its home in this desert area; it was man. Thousands of years ago, some of the southwest's earliest human inhabitants lived in the fertile valley that existed in the Pinto Basin. These early people made their home along the river that flowed through this valley. Projectile points and stone tools found at the homesites of these primitive people serve as pieces to a puzzle of a culture long past.

Millenniums after these early people and the river disappeared, Native Americans used the park area as a hunting ground and seasonal home. Remnants of their presence — projectile points, pottery, and petroglyphs — have been found throughout the park. Two tribes, the Serrano and the Chemehuevi, made a permanent home at the Oasis of Mara, part of the present-day park. When white settlers arrived, this oasis provided a place of peaceful coexistence for both American Indians and pioneers.

The late 1800's brought the first white settlers to the southern California Desert. Cattlemen, miners, and other pioneers made a home and life in and around what is now the park. Cattlemen grazed their herds on desert grasses and built water-holding tanks. The tanks were constructed by building small dams of rock and cement across the width of a wash. Rain run-off collected behind the walls and provided water for cattle during dry periods. Today these tanks can be found throughout the park. Although there are still a few that retain water, most of the tanks have since filled with sand.

The discovery of gold brought a different emphasis to the use of the land. Mines, mills, and small mining towns sprang up throughout the desert. Most of the mines within the park were worked until profits could no longer be gained. Then man moved on leaving the desert to heal its scars.

One man that didn't move on was William F. Keys. Keys arrived about 1910 and soon after began to build his lifetime home within the current boundaries of the park. He raised a family on the Desert Queen Ranch where he grew crops, grazed cattle, and worked nearby mines and mills. Even after Joshua Tree National Monument was established, Keys continued to live on his beloved ranch until his death in 1969. (Over the years, much of the ranch has slowly deteriorated. However, the National Park Service has begun recent work to restore the ranch to its former character. Today visitors can see the ranch by taking scheduled tours with a Ranger Naturalist. Take the ranch tour to experience this authentic testimony to the pioneer way of life.)

By the early 1900's, the number of people visiting the California Desert was increasing dramatically. Unfortunately, damage to the desert was increasing even more dramatically. People were removing large amounts of cacti for transplant into home cactus gardens. Visitors burned Joshua trees as nighttime street lights.

In the late 1920's, Mrs. Minerva Hoyt recognized these problems and began a crusade to save the desert. Her proposal to protect the southern California Desert as a park or monument was enthusiastically received by President Franklin Roosevelt. In 1936 a 825,000 acre monument was established. (As a result of mining pressure in 1950, the size of the monument was reduced to 560,000 acres.) Thanks to the insight of Mrs. Hoyt, a part of the southern California desert has been preserved so all may continue to explore and enjoy this desert wilderness.

In 1994, the subject of protecting the southern California Desert again came to federal government attention. Congress passed a bill that changed the status of this protected desert area from a monument to a park. The bill added 234,000 acres to the park, bringing the park to its present size of 794,000 acres. (The main difference between a national park and a national monument is the means in which the area is established. National monuments can be created by presidential proclamation. Only Congress can establish a national park.)

Some unknowing people consider the desert a wasteland. Perhaps Joshua Tree National Park may appear a wasteland to those who are not willing to explore the desert's abounding life, its colorful history, and subtle, yet sometimes profound beauty. However, those who are willing to explore and discover the park will find a special magic and life within the open valleys, secluded canyons, and high mountains. They will know this desert as a treasure to be explored, cherished, and protected. Given time, Joshua Tree National Park is certain to become a special place that finds its way to the heart.

Chapter 2
GENERAL INFORMATION

The following information will be useful as a reference both for new visitors to Joshua Tree National Park and for returning visitors.

Weather

Throughout most of the year, the park has a very favorable climate for hiking. In fact, the weather seems ideal with an average maximum temperature of 82.9°F, average minimum temperature of 51.7°F, average precipitation of 4.37" a year, and an average of 259 clear days per year. However, there are times of the year when conditions are not desirable for hiking. Temperatures in midsummer will often climb over 100° F. During these times, hiking is not advised in the lower, open areas such as Pinto Basin. Thunderstorms and downpours usually occur during July and August. These storms sometimes precipitate flash floods — a serious danger of which hikers should be wary.

Winter months may bring occasional accumulations of snow in the higher portions of the park. Usually the snow completely melts in one or two days. Snow or no snow, park visitors should be prepared for radical temperature extremes between night and day. Throughout the winter there may be several days of T-shirt weather. When the sun sets, however, the temperature quickly drops, and warm jackets and sweaters become a necessity.

The wind can sometimes be quite bothersome, especially during the cooler months of the year. Wind velocities may exceed 25 - 35 mph. This is not necessarily time to give up on hiking, but perhaps it is time to seek a sheltered route.

The following data compiled by the National Park Service will aid in preparing for hikes at different times of the year. These weather readings were taken at Park Headquarters in Twentynine Palms at an elevation of 1,960 feet. Temperatures at the higher elevations in the park will average about 10-11° F less. Precipitation at the higher altitudes will average about 3.5" more annually.

Month	Average Max. °F	Average Min. °F	Average Precipitation	Average Humidity
January	62.0	35.1	.49	30.7
February	67.2	38.3	.31	25.0
March	72.5	42.0	.35	21.2
April	80.7	48.9	.10	17.8
May	89.9	56.6	.07	14.6
June	99.1	64.2	.02	13.2
July	104.7	71.5	.66	17.9
August	102.8	70.2	.73	20.0
September	96.7	63.4	.46	17.2
October	84.5	52.7	.36	19.9
November	71.2	41.5	.31	29.9
December	63.1	36.0	.51	35.8

Camping

Six campgrounds, collectively containing almost 300 sites, are available on a first-come-first-served basis. In addition, there are about 200 reservable sites at Black Rock and Indian Cove campgrounds. Twenty-two reservable group campsites are available at Cottonwood, Indian Cove, and Sheep Pass. Reserve campsites by calling 1-800-365-CAMP.

Five of the first-come-first-served campgrounds (Hidden Valley, Ryan, Jumbo Rocks, Belle, White Tank) charge a minimal registration fee (currently $5). No water is available in these campgrounds, and the only toilet facilities are vault toilets. There are picnic tables and fire grates in all sites.

Two campgrounds, Cottonwood and Black Rock, have water and flush toilets and charge a higher fee. Indian Cove also charges a higher fee; however, it has vault toilets and no water. Water is available at the nearby Indian Cove Ranger Station. There are no hookups anywhere in the park.

Usually all campgrounds will fill on warm weekends starting on Labor Day weekend and continuing through Memorial Day weekend. All campgrounds are subject to summer seasonal closures. Call the park for up-to-date information on closures and availability.

Facilities

Other than campgrounds and picnic areas, there are no facilities within the park. (There is an emergency phone near Hidden Valley Campground.) The towns of Joshua Tree, Twentynine Palms, and Yucca Valley, along the north boundary of the park, and Chiriaco Summit, along the south boundary of the park, provide the nearest locations for gas, stores, lodging, and dining.

Visitor Centers and Ranger Stations

Water, assistance, and information may be obtained at the Oasis Visitor Center, Cottonwood Visitor Center, Indian Cove Ranger Station, Black Rock Ranger Station, and West Entrance Station. Water is also available in the Cottonwood and Black Rock campgrounds. It is not available at any other location within the park. Information is additionally available at the North Entrance Station. All visitor centers, ranger stations, and entrance stations are subject to seasonal closures. The Oasis Visitor Center in Twentynine Palms and the Cottonwood Visitor Center are the exceptions. They are open year round, seven days a week.

General Regulations

The following regulations should be helpful to those not familiar with National Park Service areas. This is only a partial list containing commonly overlooked or misunderstood rules. Contact a ranger or inquire at a visitor center if there are any questions about regulations.

- No weapons of any kind are allowed within the park. This includes paint ball guns, BB guns, slingshots, and bows & arrows.

- All vegetation, dead or alive, is protected and therefore may not be collected or burned.

- All wildlife (including snakes and scorpions) is protected and therefore may not be killed, harassed, collected, or fed.

- Pets must be kept leashed. They are not allowed in the backcountry or on any trails except the Oasis of Mara.

- Vehicles, including bicycles, are permitted only on established roads.

- Camping is allowed only in designated campgrounds and in the backcountry. (See Chapter 3 for information on backcountry regulations.)

- A permit is required for camping in the backcountry.

- All cultural artifacts are protected. It is prohibited to collect, disturb, or remove any historical or prehistoric artifact.

For additional information, call or write:

Joshua Tree National Park
74485 National Park Drive
Twentynine Palms, CA 92277
(760) 367-5500
Website: www.nps.gov/jotr

Chapter 3
HIKING INFORMATION FOR JOSHUA TREE NATIONAL PARK

Hiking in Joshua Tree National Park is different from hiking in other commonly hiked areas around the country. The information contained in this chapter should be helpful for recognizing and preparing for these differences.

Route Selection Tips

Many of the hikes in this book do not have an official trail. Most of these hikes follow washes, canyons, valleys, ridges, and closed dirt roads. The following tips should be helpful both when following the hike descriptions and when venturing into undescribed areas.

- If there are no roads or trails, it is generally easier to travel in the washes and along ridges rather than through the open desert. Use of these travel aids eliminates time-consuming zigzagging around vegetation.

- Old dirt roads closed to vehicle traffic are another travel aid. However, be advised that time has erased many of the dirt roads marked on the earlier topographic maps.

- Distance can be deceiving in the wide open spaces of the desert. What appears to be a short walk away may be hours away and visa versa. Use a topographical map to determine distances.

- Many desert landmarks look similar. Study and take note of your surroundings for the return trip. Keep track of your location on a topographical map.

Planning & Preparing

The following information is provided to aid with the planning and preparing for both day and overnight hikes.

Backcountry Registration: All overnight backcountry users must register before heading into the backcountry. Backpackers may obtain a non-fee permit at any of the twelve backcountry boards located throughout the park. The backpacking group carries the top half of the permit with them. The bottom half of the permit is deposited at the board. A backcountry board parking area is the only place a vehicle may be left overnight. Park employees may grant exceptions to this rule.

Special Equipment: The following are some equipment needs for desert hiking.

- For overnight and full day trips, clothing is needed for both temperature extremes — warm days and cold nights.

- A hat, sunglasses and sunscreen are recommended to protect against the bright desert sun.

- For off-trail hikes, long pants are desirable to protect against rough desert brush.

- Good walking shoes or tennis shoes are adequate for the easier hikes. Sturdy, lightweight hiking boots, which provide good ankle support, are recommended for the more rugged hikes.

- A map, compass, and orienteering skills are recommended for all but the most straightforward trail hikes (i.e., nature trails).

Water: Water in the backcountry is found in only a few places and only at certain times of the year. Never depend upon finding a natural water source unless first hand information is available. Even then, a natural water source should not be the primary source of water. Before drinking any water from these areas, purify the water. During the warm parts of the year, each hiker should plan to carry at least one gallon of water per day. (Freeze-dried food is not recommended for desert use because of the need for extra water.)

Fragile Environment — Rules and Ethics: The backcountry of the park bares few scars of overuse or misuse (disregarding mining scars). To keep it this way, hikers and backpackers need to follow both the park regulations and the Minimum Impact Ethic: Hike and enjoy the park, but leave the park in its natural and undisturbed state so others that follow may enjoy the same.

The following are National Park Service regulations and guidelines that keep within this ethic.

- <u>Trail use and route selection</u>: Hike on trails whenever possible. When hiking through areas that have no trails, travel in the sandy washes, on rocky ground, or in other unvegetated areas. Unthoughtful route selection can result in destruction of the thin desert-soil crust, trampling of delicate vegetation, erosion, and creation of unnecessary trails. It can take more than a hundred years for the soil and vegetation of the fragile desert to recover from careless human impact.

- <u>Campsite selection</u>: There are no established backcountry campgrounds. Each hiking party selects a campsite at their discretion while considering a few site selection rules. (This is the current Joshua Tree National Park policy and is subject to change. Check on existing policies before planning an overnight trip.) Do not camp within one mile of any road nor within 500 feet of any trail. Set up tents in areas having little or no vegetation. (Be aware of the flash flood danger when camping near a wash.) Campsites must be at least 200 feet from any water source. This will prevent pollution of this limited resource and permit access for wildlife. Do not level sites, dig trenches, or build rock structures. This causes soil disturbance and leaves visible signs of human presence.

- <u>Fires</u>: No open fires are allowed in the backcountry due to the danger of wildfire. Campfires scar and sterilize the soil. Their remains create an eyesore. Self-contained backpacking stoves are recommended.

- <u>Garbage and litter</u>: Carry all garbage and litter out of the backcountry. Buried refuse is usually dug up by animals and scattered by the wind. Any substance foreign to the desert such as garbage, orange peels, cigarette butts, and paper will take years to decompose in the arid environment. (Do not remove "historical litter" — i.e., equipment, cans, etc., left by pioneers and miners.)

- <u>Human waste</u>: Dispose of human feces in catholes, small holes dug about 6" deep. Cover the holes with soil and make the area look as natural as possible. Catholes should be at least 200 feet from any water source. Pack out all toilet paper in a plastic bag rather than burying or burning it.

- Water source: Never wash in or near a water source. Conserve water from these natural sources. Remember, wildlife depend upon this water for survival.

- Day use areas: Certain areas in the park are restricted to day use. (Refer to the section "Understanding Day Use Areas...," page 23.) Before backpacking near one of these areas, go to a visitor center and have the restricted area outlined on a topographical map. As an alternative, use the map drawings and topographical maps in this book to aid in identifying the boundaries of the day use areas. (See Chapter 4, Maps.)

Hazards - Use Caution

Hikers might be exposed to the following dangers while traveling in the park. Observing the suggested precautions could keep an enjoyable hike from becoming an unpleasant or even tragic experience.

Mines and Buildings: Mines and building ruins provide an interesting historical emphasis to hikes; they also provide a potential hazard. Never consider a mine shaft safe for entry. The shafts are composed mainly of crumbling unsupported rock. The timber shoring is rotten. Vertical mine shafts are especially dangerous since the ground surrounding the shaft's opening may be undercut and weak. Some of these shafts drop straight down hundreds of feet. Wooden building structures are also unsafe for entry due to rotting wood. Enjoy and explore the mines and buildings but only on the outside.

Flash Floods: Heavy rains, even for short periods, may create flash floods in mountain or hilly areas. Flash floods most commonly occur during July and August but may occur during any period of heavy rain. To avoid this danger, keep alert to weather conditions. Don't camp or hike in canyons and washes during rainy periods. Never attempt to cross a flooded wash; the water level is apt to rise quickly and with little warning.

Snakes and Other Misunderstoods: The California Desert is home to many varieties of snakes, scorpions, spiders, lizards, and insects. Certain species of these creatures deserve respect and caution, but probably not the amount of fear they usually instill.

- Snakes: There are six varieties of rattlesnakes within the park. These snakes are not aggressive. They do provide a danger when they are provoked, surprised or stepped on. Use caution when stepping down off an overhanging rock or when walking through bushes. During the hot part of the day, snakes stay in the shade under bushes and rocks. In the cooler evening, they prefer open roads or washes. They hibernate during the winter, usually between November and early March.

- <u>Lizards</u>: There are no known poisonous lizards in the park.

- <u>Scorpions</u>: The sting of a scorpion (native species) may be painful. However, it is potentially fatal only if the person stung has a severe allergic reaction. Centruroides, the most poisonous of scorpions, is not known to inhabit the park.

- <u>Spiders</u>: Tarantulas (native species) are commonly active in the spring, summer, and fall months. Although they are big and scary looking, they cause little harm. They are docile, relatively slow, and only mildly poisonous. Black Widow spiders are poisonous and do live in the park. However, they are not aggressive and their bite is seldom fatal.

A few common sense rules and precautions will help prevent any undesirable encounters with the above creatures. Look carefully before sitting and before placing feet or hands. Keep garbage away from camp areas. Keep campsites clean; food crumbs attract insects and small animals that, in turn, are food for scorpions, spiders, and snakes. Shake out all bedding and clothing before using.

Vicious Plants: Certain plants in the park are responsible for many more inflictions than all the snakes and spiders combined. The thorns of a catsclaw, the pointed unyielding spikes of the yucca, and the barbed spines of the cholla all deserve caution and avoidance. Unintentional contact with these plants can leave a hiker tending to annoying and painful wounds.

Weather Related Medical Emergencies: Due to the temperature extremes, hikers could be presented with medical emergencies such as heat exhaustion, heat stroke, or hypothermia. Be aware of these potential problems, know their signs and symptoms, and know how to treat them.

Understanding Day Use Areas and Desert Bighorn Sheep

The desert bighorn, a rare subspecies of bighorn sheep, survives in small numbers in isolated places throughout the Southwest. Joshua Tree National Park supports a small population of these animals. The bighorns' prime habitat in the park is within the day use areas. It is in these areas that the sheep can find the rugged terrain, isolation, and water pockets that are essential for their survival.

The sheep in Joshua Tree are very shy and nervous. Disturbances to their living patterns will cause them to become physically run-down. Under stress, they cease to reproduce. For these reasons, it is most important that all human visitation to day use areas be kept to solely daylight hours. This will allow the sheep to roam undisturbed at night and make their way to water sources.

Camping in a day use area or by a water hole will not enhance the chances of seeing a bighorn. It will only keep the sheep away from the area and the water on which they depend. In turn the sheep may weaken and with continued disturbance may die. **Please do not contribute to the decline of the desert bighorn sheep; camp outside of day use areas.**

Chapter 4
USING THIS GUIDE

The hikes described in this book are divided into chapters covering twelve different areas in the park. This will aid in choosing day hikes near a frontcountry campground basecamp. Information contained in this chapter and in the appendixes at the end of the book will help clarify the individual hike descriptions.

A data reference list precedes each hike description. To interpret this data accurately, refer to the section in this chapter entitled "Guide Description Explanations." References are made to landmarks and starting and ending points in all hike descriptions. Refer to Appendix A, "Landmark Descriptions and Directions."

Hike, explore, and enjoy Joshua Tree National Park!

Maps

Map drawings that show the relationship of hikes to roads, campgrounds, and backcountry boards are provided for each hiking area. The drawings are helpful for choosing and preparing for a hike; however, they are not a substitute for a topographical map. The map key, on the following page, applies to the map drawings and topographical maps located throughout the book.

Day use areas on the map drawings are depicted by thin lines and squares. The squares correspond to numbered sections (outlined in red) on USGS topographical maps. They may be used to help transpose the day use areas onto USGS maps.

The Wonderland Day Use Area follows geographical features and not section lines. Because of the irregular boundaries, it is difficult to plot this day use area on the line maps in this book. The following description may prove helpful: Start at the north boundary of the park, one mile west of the

Map Key

All Maps		Drawn Maps Only

▲ Campgrounds   ━━━ Paved Roads   ☐ Day Use Areas

〻 Picnic Areas   ━·━ Dirt Roads

         ----- Trails &   ▨ Restricted Areas
                Road-trails

B Backcountry   ······ Cross-country   ▬ Park Boundary
    Boards   routes

? Visitor Centers/   ▬▬ Day Use Areas   Ⓗ Hike destinations
    Information

Indian Cove Road. The day use boundary leads south along the Boy Scout Trail to the Boy Scout Trailhead on Park Boulevard. Follow the roads from the backcountry board, to Echo T, and on to O'Dell Parking Area. Continue east along the south base of Queen Mountain over to Pine City. Continue down the canyon past Pine Springs to the North Entrance. From the North Entrance, follow the park boundary north to Base Line Road then west back to the start. If there is any question about day use area boundaries, inquire at a ranger station or visitor center.

In Appendix D, there are topographical maps that cover almost all the hikes. (Note that day use areas are identified.) The 15' maps do not provide enough detail for locating good landmarks on cross-country hikes. However, they can be used to identify and transpose routes and day use areas onto 7.5' maps.

The more detailed 7.5' topographical maps may be obtained at the Oasis, Cottonwood, and Black Rock visitor centers. The use of 7.5' topographical maps is recommended for cross-country hikes. The names of 7.5' USGS maps are listed in the information preceding each hike.

Another useful map that can be purchased at the information centers is the Trails Illustrated Topo Map. This smaller scale topographical map covers the entire park and has many of the hikes outlined on the map.

Compass Directions

In this guide, all compass headings written in the form of numbers or letters (i.e., 25°, NW) are field bearings or magnetic north readings. Written directions (i.e., north) refer to general true north directions.

Guide Description Explanations

The following explains the terms used in the list of pertinent facts that precedes each hike.

Type: Each route is described by one of the following terms:

- trail — a foot trail that is maintained by the National Park Service

- road-trail — a dirt road that was created before the park was established. It is closed to vehicle traffic but still provides a route of travel for the hiker.

- cross-country (x/country) — a hike that uses no man-made travel aids. It may consist of a combination of hiking in washes, along ridges, or through open desert.

- Recommendations are made for conducting the hike as a day or an overnight trip. A hike is not recommended for an overnight trip if it leads to a day use area or if it starts in an area where there is no backcountry board.

Mileage: Mileage is round trip unless otherwise noted.

Time: All time estimates are based upon the time it takes an average hiker to leisurely complete the trip.

Difficulty: This addresses the strenuousness (first four terms) and technical difficulty (last three terms) of the terrain. Distance is not considered. All hikes are given a rating for strenuousness. Only some hikes are given a rating for difficulty. Consider hikes with no difficulty rating as having little or no difficulty.

- easy — generally level or gentle downhill terrain

- moderate — involves a limited amount of uphill and downhill travel

- moderately strenuous — involves quite a bit of uphill and downhill travel; terrain provides easier walking than strenuous hikes

- strenuous — mostly uphill and downhill travel with rocky footing

- moderately difficult — involves rocky places where some boulder hopping and scrambling is necessary

- difficult — involves many rocky areas and difficult boulder hopping and scrambling

- difficult (+) — involves extreme boulder scrambling or areas where some technical rock climbing ability is recommended

Elevation Extremes: the lowest and highest points over which a trail or route travels

Starting and Ending Points: Within the park, there are few directional signs relating to the backcountry. Use Appendix A, "Landmark Descriptions and Directions" to obtain specific directions on how to reach the listed starting and ending points for each hike.

Topographic Diagrams: For most of the hikes in this book, it is easy to judge the strenuousness and character of the hike by taking note of the elevation extremes and differences. However, some hikes involve repeated up and down traveling. This makes the stated elevation difference somewhat meaningless. Topographic diagrams, such as the one below, are provided for these particular hikes. The diagrams reflect the total elevation gained and lost throughout the hike.

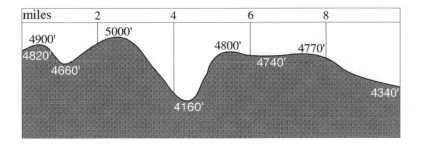

Chapter 5
NATURE TRAILS

Throughout the park there are several short trails ranging from 0.2 to 1.7 miles in length. These trails travel along gentle terrain and lead to some of the highlights of the park. Along each trail there are interpretive signs that point out the important natural and historical aspects of the area.

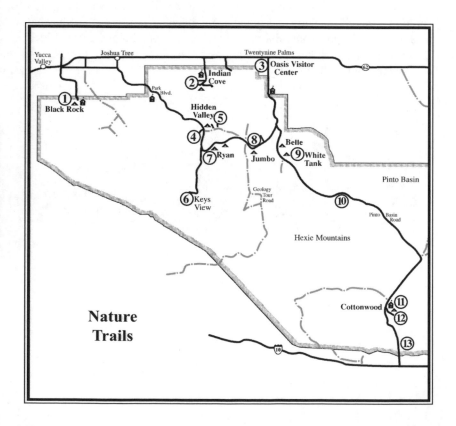

1. HIGH VIEW

Mileage: 1.3 mile loop
Difficulty: moderate
Starting Point: South Park
Parking Area / Black Rock

Appendix D Map: # 5

Summary: This moderately steep trail leads to a good viewpoint of the town of Yucca Valley and Mt. San Gorgonio, an 11,499' peak located in the San Bernardino Mountains. Mt. San Gorgonio, with its winter mantle of snow, provides a beautiful contrast with the desert mountains that surround High View.

Take advantage of the benches located at several points along the trail. Rest, enjoy the scenery, and study the varied vegetation of the Mojave Desert. Watch lizards and small animals scurry around.

Numbered posts point out the highlights along the trail. Obtain the corresponding interpretive handout at the Black Rock Visitor Center. The handout provides interesting information on plant adaptations in a high desert environment and explains animal relationships with these plants.

The loop is designed for clockwise travel. From the parking lot, the trail leads over a short flat section before beginning the steady 355' ascent to the ridgetop. There is a trail register and bench at the high point on the trail. The equally steady descent leads down a drainage to gentler ground. The last 1/4 mile is fairly level.

This trail can also be accessed from Black Rock Campground. A spur trail, which begins west of the ranger station, travels 1/2 mile along the base of the hills. It intersects the nature trail 150 yards south of the parking lot.

2. INDIAN COVE

Mileage: 0.6 mile loop
Difficulty: easy
Starting Point: Indian Cove Campground, west end

Appendix D Map: # 7

Summary: Indian Cove is nestled among the large monzogranite boulder piles on the northern edge of the Wonderland of Rocks. The Nature Trail skirts the edge of the boulders and travels through low hills and a wide sandy wash. Signs along the way identify plants, explain plant uses by early Indians, discuss plant and animal relationships, and touch on the natural life of a Mojave Desert wash.

While traveling the trail, look for signs of bighorn sheep. Although the sheep are elusive, they are occasionally seen traveling on the rugged formations within the Wonderland. Watch for their silhouette upon a rocky peak.

The nature trail can also be accessed from the group campground between sites 12 and 13. From the group sites, this spur trail travels 1/8 mile and joins the main trail at the most northern section of the loop.

3. OASIS OF MARA (Twentynine Palms Oasis)

Mileage: 0.5 mile loop   **Mileage with extension:** 1.5 mile loop
Difficulty: easy, accessible by wheelchair
Starting Point: Oasis Visitor Center

Summary: The Oasis of Mara has been a center of life throughout the history of man's presence in the Southern California Desert. Two tribes of American Indians, the Serrano and the Chemehuevi, initially inhabited the oasis. Later, prospectors and homesteaders moved into the area. When white settlers arrived, this oasis provided a place of peaceful coexistence for both the Indians and the pioneers. Today the only reminder of man's historical presence at the oasis is the gravestone of a young woman who died in 1903. All dwellings and other signs of human habitation have long since vanished.

A paved loop trail circles beneath the rustling palms. Signs along the trail interpret the plants, animals, history and geology of the area. A pamphlet, obtained at the start of the trail, provides additional information on the history and the natural life of this miniature ecosystem.

A dirt trail, known as the Oasis Trail Extension, leaves from the back side of the loop and leads to the Twentynine Palms Art Gallery, the Historical Society Museum, and the Twentynine Palms

Inn. Numbered posts along the trail point out different plants and area highlights. Ask for the accompanying handout at the visitor center.

4. HIDDEN VALLEY

Mileage: 1 mile loop   **Appendix D Map:** # 7
Difficulty: easy
Starting Point: Hidden Valley Picnic Area, westside parking lot

Summary: Legend suggests that this rock-enclosed valley was a hideout for cattle and horse rustlers in the late 1800's. Rocky walls and massive boulder piles create a natural corral that could have contained stolen cattle and horses.

Today, a narrow gap in the rocks provides the only easy entrance into the valley. Bill Keys, one of the early desert pioneers, created this gap in 1936. Keys blasted the opening into the valley to improve access for his legitimate cattle operation. (To learn more about the interesting life of Bill Keys, ask a park ranger about Desert Queen Ranch Tours.)

The trail leaves the parking lot, passes through the narrow gap, and circles the perimeter of the valley. Joshua trees, those tall, spiny trees that are characteristic of the Mojave Desert, are scattered throughout the valley.

Large oaks and pines grow in the shade of the valley's rocky walls. Signs along the trail discuss these plants and interpret other plants and animals supported by the valley's microclimate. Some signs discuss plant uses by early desert Indians, while others touch on recent human impacts to the area.

Hidden Valley is a popular area for sport climbing. Look for rock climbers on the many rock formations around the perimeter and in the middle of the valley. While scanning the rocks for climbers, watch for the rock formation known as the Trojan (pictured right). This unusual face profile is near the northeast corner of the loop.

5. BARKER DAM

Mileage: 1.3 mile loop
Difficulty: easy
Starting Point: Barker Dam
Parking Area

Appendix D Map: # 7

Summary: This hike is located in one of the few easily accessible areas of the Wonderland. Early cowboys originally built Barker Dam to collect water for cattle. Later, Pioneer Bill Keys added an additional six vertical feet to the dam. Keys renamed it "Bighorn Dam" and etched this new name into the cement. Today the dam retains a small, beautiful lake framed by the rugged boulders of the Wonderland. (Water levels are dependent upon the annual rainfall and the time of year.)

Bill Keys also built the unusual watering trough below the dam. He designed the trough to conserve water, a precious desert resource. The center ring in the trough protected a float device that prevented the water from overflowing.

The trail leads past the lake and dam. It loops around Piano Valley then returns to the parking lot. Signs along the way cover two themes. Near the lake, the signs interpret the plant and bird life surrounding a desert water source. These signs additionally address historical uses of the water by early Indians and pioneers. Along other sections of the trail, the signs interpret the plants and animals of the Mojave Desert and explain their adaptations for a dry environment.

Notice the large boulder to the right of the trail in Piano Valley. With imagination this rock, appropriately named Piano Rock, looks like a huge grand piano. However, it was named for another reason. In the late 1930's, local residents organized musical camping trips to this area. According to Willis Keys, then a young local resident, the campers placed a piano on top of the boulder. They would then sit on Joshua tree logs and listen to a concert. Note the weathered gray logs still lined up at the base of the boulder.

At the southwest corner of the loop, a short side trip leads to some petroglyphs located in an elevated rock overhang. The site is 100 feet south on a side trail. Watch for the signs.

Petroglyphs are designs chipped into the rocks by early Native Americans. Experts who study petroglyphs are still uncertain whether the carvings were a form of communication or just doodling. A film crew unfortunately painted over some of these petroglyphs in an attempt to make the carvings more visible. A few of the carvings located on the base of the overhang remain undamaged.

6. KEYS VIEW LOOP

Mileage: 0.25 mile loop   **Appendix D Map:** # 9
Difficulty: easy
Starting Point: Keys View

Summary: Keys View sits on the crest of the Little San Bernardino Mountains. It is the highest point in the park that can be reached by paved road. The area is well known for its spectacular view of the Coachella Valley, Mt. San Jacinto, Mt. San Gorgonio, and the Salton Sea. A short paved trail ascends steeply to a high viewpoint of these landmarks and several other points of interest — the Santa Rosa Mts., Indio, Palm Springs, the San Andreas Fault, and Signal Mt. in Mexico (90 miles to the south). Viewing benches and large interpretive signs are spaced along the loop trail.

The panorama is outstanding; however, a haze frequently diminishes the view. The pollution, which rolls in from the Los Angeles metropolis, has become increasingly more evident over the past several years. It has become so evident that the National Park Service has installed a sign addressing differing smog levels. Generally there will be less smog on calmer, cooler days. Additionally, visibility is usually better after a hard rain.

7. CAP ROCK

Mileage: 0.4 mile loop   **Appendix D Map:** # 9
Difficulty: easy, accessible by wheelchair
Starting Point: Cap Rock Parking Area

Summary: A natural curiosity that exists within this portion of the park is the unique collection of gigantic boulder piles. The Cap Rock Formation is one of these unusual piles of stone. A large rock perched like a cap on top of a massive pile of boulders prompted the naming of this rock formation.

A level, paved trail leaves Cap Rock (pictured left) and circles through smaller boulder formations. Signs along the trail identify the plants and explain relationships between the plants and Mojave Desert wildlife. Some signs explain plant adaptations for surviving in a desert environment.

Cap Rock is a popular climbing area. Watch for climbers on the Cap Rock Formation as well as on the smaller formations along the trail.

8. SKULL ROCK

Mileage: 1.7 mile loop
Difficulty: easy
Starting Point: Jumbo Rocks Campground, middle of the campground on the main campground road

Appendix D Map: # 8

Summary: This trail meanders through boulders, desert washes, and a rocky alleyway. Interpretive signs along the trail identify plants, explain the geology of the Mojave Desert, discuss plant and animal relationships, and describe plant uses by early Native Americans. The trail leads to Skull Rock (pictured right), an unusual rock formation that can be viewed from the trail as well as from the road. The large monzogranite boulder is shaped in likeness to a gigantic human skull. Large concave depressions form the skull's eye sockets and nostrils.

Access the trail from one of three locations: the entrance to Jumbo Rocks Campground; the middle of the campground; or at Skull Rock, a pullout located a short distance east of the campground entrance. The recommended and described starting point is the trailhead in the middle of the campground.

The trail travels 1/2 mile from the campground to Skull Rock. The interpretive signs are located on this first portion of the trail. At Skull Rock, the trail crosses the road and continues on the other side. It travels through rocky alleys and climbs along a boulder slab as it leads to the campground entrance. The last 0.4 miles of the loop follow the campground road back to the trailhead.

9. ARCH ROCK

Mileage: 0.3 mile loop   **Appendix D Map:** # 8
Difficulty: easy
Starting Point: White Tank Campground, near Site # 9

Summary: Signs along this trail explain the geology of the area and the natural creation of an arch. It took the forces of nature many years to create Arch Rock out of a monzogranite boulder pile. The arch spans a 35' distance and rises about 15' above the underlying boulder. The trail travels to Arch Rock, circles through a rocky area, then exits near the end of the campground. Complete the loop by following the campground road back to the trailhead.

A short side trip through narrow alleys formed by rock monoliths leads to White Tank. In the early 1900's, cattlemen constructed this tank by building a small dam of rock and cement across the width of the wash. Rain runoff collected behind the wall and provided water for cattle. Like most of the many other tanks in the park, White Tank has since filled with sand. However, it still provides a moist, verdant area attractive to birds and wildlife. Large boulders and natural crawlways fill the wash above the tank.

No trail leads to White Tank; the hike involves route finding and some rock scrambling. To find the tank, leave the trail at the Arch Rock exhibit sign and scramble up the boulders to the front of the arch. Continue past the arch through a narrow alley bordered by boulders on both sides. About 65 yards from the arch, the alley leads along the base of a large boulder about 40' high. Scramble down through the alley past this boulder. Look left and find another large boulder with a passage under it. Climb through the passage to reach the top of the tank.

10. CHOLLA CACTUS GARDEN

Mileage: 0.25 mile loop   **Appendix D Map: # 3**
Difficulty: easy
Starting Point: Pinto Basin Road, near mile 10, southeast side of road

Summary: This trail travels through an unusually dense concentration of Bigelow cholla, a plant characteristic to the Colorado Desert. From a distance, the Bigelow cholla looks soft and fuzzy and hence has gained the name teddy bear cholla. However, a close look at this plant will reveal the true identity of the Bigelow. Fine bristles cover each plant, and each bristle has a microscopic barb on the exposed end. Even brushing lightly against a cholla can cause the spines to penetrate and stick to skin and clothing.

Cholla Cactus Garden sits on the lower edge of the transition zone between the Mojave and Colorado deserts. The Joshua trees of the Mojave Desert do not extend to this lower elevation. Instead, there is an abundance of large bushy creosote, a predominate plant in the Colorado Desert.

This trail provides a place to examine and learn about the natural life of the Colorado Desert. A self-guiding pamphlet is available at the parking lot.

11. BOTANICAL WALK

Mileage: 0.2 mile loop
Difficulty: easy
Starting Point: Cottonwood Visitor Center

Summary: This short trail system loops through typical Colorado Desert vegetation. Signs along the way identify the plants.

12. COTTONWOOD

Mileage: 1.4 miles (round-trip)   **Appendix D Map: # 11**
Difficulty: easy
Starting Point: Cottonwood Campground, sites 13A & 13B or Cottonwood Springs (The hike is described starting from the campground.)

Summary: The Cottonwood Nature Trail provides an opportunity to explore the Colorado Desert and learn about its early human inhabitants. Long before the park was established, Cahuilla Indians inhabited the oases and springs in the southern park area. These people were well adapted to desert living. They thrived by making use of the many plants and animals of the Colorado Desert.

The Cottonwood Nature Trail passes through the rolling hills of the Colorado Desert as it travels from the campground to Cottonwood Spring. Signs along the trail interpret the plants and animals and explain how the Cahuilla Indians used the plants in their daily lives.

Cottonwood Spring is a significant water source, sometimes producing up to 30 gallons an hour. The thick collection of palm trees and cottonwoods provides important habitat for wildlife in the area. The spring was an important water source for people between the years of 1870-1910. It was one of the few water sources located along the popular route of travel between Mecca and the Dale Mining District. Pick up the park brochure entitled "A Day at Cottonwood Spring" to learn more about the area. Be sure to look for the mining arrastra and Indian bedrock mortar (pictured above), both found on the east side of the wash near the spring.

Start the hike from either trailhead in the campground. The two trails join together within a short distance. About 0.4 miles from the trailhead, there is a junction in a major wash. Go to the right. Traveling to the left leads to the Winona Mill Site (Chapter 15, Hike # 7). The nature trail ends a short distance past the spring.

13. BAJADA TRAIL

New Hike

Mileage: 0.25 mile loop
Difficulty: easy
Starting Point: parking lot on east side of Pinto Basin Road, 5.5 miles south of Cottonwood Visitor Center, 1.5 miles north of Interstate 10

Summary: This hard-surfaced trail explores the natural life on a desert bajada. A bajada is a long slope composed of the eroded sand and gravel from nearby mountains. Signs along the trail interpret the plant and animal life of this bajada. Three benches spaced along the trail provide a place to relax and enjoy the area.

This trail was specially designed as an all-access trail for the physically impaired. The hard surface is appropriate for wheelchairs. For the visually impaired, there are raised tactile strips along the trail denoting the points of interest. An audio tape and tape deck, which you can borrow from the Cottonwood Visitor Center, explains these points of interest.

Chapter 6
PARK BOULEVARD EAST

The eastern half of Park Boulevard travels from the Oasis Visitor Center in Twentynine Palms to Sheep Pass in the center of the park. The road travels up a large alluvial fan, passes among rugged monzogranite boulders, then continues through Queen Valley to Sheep Pass. Several short, pleasant hikes, as well as longer and more difficult hikes, start from this road. The North Entrance Backcountry Board is 0.5 miles inside the entrance. Nearby campgrounds include Jumbo Rocks, located 12 miles from park headquarters and four miles east of Sheep Pass. Belle and White Tank campgrounds are located a few miles south on Pinto Basin Road.

1. OASIS OF MARA - (See Chapter 5, Hike # 3.)

2. JOSHUA MOUNTAIN (Indian Head) (3746')

Type: x-country, day
Mileage: 2.6 miles (round-trip)
Time: 2 - 3 hours
Difficulty: strenuous, difficult
Elevation Extremes: 2570' - 3746'   **Difference:** 1176'
Starting and Ending Point: Utah Trail, 2.5 miles S of Oasis Visitor Center (2570')
Topo Maps: Queen Mtn. 7.5'   **Appendix D Map:** # 8

Summary: Joshua Mountain is an impressive-looking peak with sheer 160' cliffs on the summit block. The shape of the summit block has prompted the nickname of Indian Head. The hike is short but difficult due to the steep, rocky terrain. From the summit, there is a panoramic view of Twentynine Palms City, the surrounding desert mountains, and the large alluvial fan that descends from the park.

Route: From the roadside parking on Utah Trail, the peak can be seen to the west. Hike up the obvious steep gully that leads to the south base of Indian Head. Go around to the north side by traveling to either side of the summit block. Scramble up to the summit via the steep north-facing slope.

PARK BOULEVARD EAST

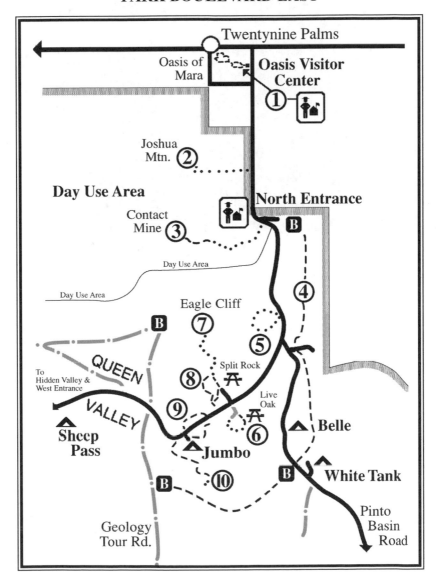

Yucca in bloom at the base of Joshua Mountain

3. CONTACT MINE

Type: road-trail / x-country, day
Mileage: 3.4 miles (round-trip)
Time: 2 - 3 hours
Difficulty: moderately strenuous
Elevation Extremes: 2920'- 3640'   **Difference:** 720'
Starting and Ending Point: North Entrance Exhibit (2920')
Topo Maps: Queen Mtn. 7.5'   **Appendix D Map:** # 8

Summary: The Contact Mine may prove noteworthy to those who have an interest in the early mining era. Building ruins, machinery, tram tracks, a cable winch, and a few partially collapsed shafts remain at this once successful mining area. The mine reportedly realized substantial profits in gold and silver in the early 1900's. (Mine shafts are dangerous; maintain a safe distance from the openings. Refer to Chapter 3, "Hazards - Use Caution.")

Route: An obscure dirt road leaves the west side of Park Boulevard about twenty-five yards north of the Entrance Exhibit. Follow the road 1/4 mile south to a dirt dike. Cross the dike and travel 50 yards to another dike, which parallels a wash. Follow the dike SW to its end then continue up the wash. Take the right fork in the wash. Continue to follow the wash as it contours around the rocky hills to the right (north). (Begin looking for a road on the lower half of the mountain to the west; it's the Contact Mine Road.)

A half mile beyond the end of the dike, the mine road leaves the right side of the wash. Watch for the road's vague beginnings at a narrow point in the wash located between two rocky hills. The first few hundred feet of the road are hard to discern. The remainder of the road is easy to follow. (Note: The road-trail to Contact Mine is not pictured on the Queen Mtn. 7.5' map; however, the mine itself is labeled.)

4. CALIFORNIA RIDING AND HIKING TRAIL
(See Chapter 11)

Cable winch at the Contact Mine

5. PINTO WYE ARRASTRA

Type: x-country, day
Mileage: 1.25 miles (round-trip) or 2 mile loop
Time: 1 hour
Difficulty: moderately strenuous (loop difficult)
Elevation Extremes: 3550' (3440') - 3740   **Difference:** 190' (300')
Starting and Ending Point: pullout on Park Blvd., 0.5 miles north of Pinto Wye
Topo Maps: Queen Mtn. 7.5'   **Appendix D Map:** # 8

Summary: The Pinto Wye Arrastra is one of only two wagon wheel arrastras found on national park lands. It is relatively well preserved. Because it provides an example of 19th and early 20th century ore-milling techniques, it has been nominated for placement on the National Register of Historic Places. A more difficult, but interesting, loop hike can be made by following the wash past the mine/mill site.

Route: Park in the circular pullout located on the east side of the road, 0.5 miles north of Pinto Wye. Head west up a gully to a pass between two roadside hills. Start down the other side of the pass and look west to locate the arrastra slightly above the east side of the wash. Either return via the same route or continue on the loop hike.

To travel the loop, follow the wash NW as it winds down a boulder canyon. Upon exiting the canyon, leave the wash to the right and travel around the base of the hill. Intersect Park Boulevard and continue to the right (south) to reach the parking area.

6. LIVE OAK / IVANPAH TANKS

Type: x-country / road-trail, day
Mileage: 1 mile loop
Time: 0.5 hour
Difficulty: easy
Elevation Extremes: relatively level
Starting and Ending Point: Live Oak Picnic Area, west end
Topo Maps: Queen Mtn. 7.5', Malapai Hill 7.5'   **Appendix D Map:** # 8

Summary: This short loop hike travels past a very large, rare hybrid oak, after which the picnic area was named. The route leads down a sandy, rock-enclosed wash to Live Oak Tank and then on to Ivanpah Tank. A tank is a watering hole found behind a man-made wall that spans the width of a wash. Ranchers built Ivanpah Tank, one of the larger tanks in the area, for cattle-raising in the early 1900's.

Unlike many of the other tanks in the park, Ivanpah holds water in the wet seasons. When the water subsides, a field of sacred daturas flourishes in the damp soil. The large trumpet shape flowers of the datura, also known as jimsonweed and thorn apple, usually bloom at night and wither in the direct sunlight. However, when there is sufficient cloud cover or shading, the flowers will continue to bloom well into the day. Spring and Fall are excellent times to view the floral display at Ivanpah. Traveling down the wash past the tank leads to more interesting rocky terrain.

Route: Follow the sandy wash south past the large oak. The first low stone wall is Live Oak Tank. Ivanpah, a much larger tank, is farther down the same wash. At Ivanpah climb the left bank, which overlooks the tank, and locate the road-trail. The road-trail leads to the east end of the picnic area. Complete the circuit by following the picnic area road back to the west end of the picnic area.

A hiker admires the large, rare oak in Live Oak Wash.

7. EAGLE CLIFF HILLS / MINE

Type: trail/x-country, day
Mileage: 2.5 miles (round-trip)
Time: 2 - 3 hours
Difficulty: strenuous, moderately difficult
Elevation Extremes: 4280' - 4620'   **Difference:** 340'
Starting and Ending Point: Split Rock Picnic Area (4280')
Topo Maps: Queen Mtn. 7.5'   **Appendix D Map:** # 4

Summary: The Eagle Cliff Hills form a beautiful and isolated wilderness fortress with rocky peaks, massive boulder piles, plentiful vegetation, and high viewpoints. Although the area is close to roads, it receives little use due to the rugged terrain. Because this area is rugged and confusing, solo travel is discouraged. Good map and compass skills are essential, especially for the return trip from the mine to Split Rock. These hills can be accessed either through Split Rock Picnic Area or through Desert Queen Mine (see Chapter 8, Hike # 10).

The Eagle Cliff Mine lies on a sheltered plateau in the heart of the Eagle Cliff Hills. The highlight of this mining area is a house built within a pile of giant boulders. The house utilizes these boulders for its walls and a portion of the roof. The remainder of the roof is constructed of dead boughs and flattened tin cans. Inside the shelter there are miscellaneous utensils, a fireplace, an iron oventop, and wooden shelves surrounding a six-pane glass window. These remnants hint about life in the early mining days.

There is little known about the history of this structure. However, the remains indicate that a small group of miners probably lived at the Eagle Cliff Mine for an extended time.

This plateau is one of many good camping spots within the Eagle Cliff Hills. Overnight users need to leave from the Pine City Backcountry Board; see Chapter 8. (Mines are dangerous; maintain a safe distance from the openings. Refer to Chapter 3, "Hazards - Use Caution.")

Route: The trail starts at Split Rock, a massive boulder that is split in two. From the parking lot, walk around the left side of Split Rock to a cave on the rock's north side. The cave is formed by the overhanging edges of the giant boulder. The trail heads north from the cave.

At 0.3 miles, there is a junction. The Split Rock Loop Trail makes a sharp left. The Eagle Cliff Route continues straight. From here, head north over some low rocky ridges to reach to a gully between two mountain points. Look for a short spire with a broad base located at the top of the gully. The spire is an important landmark for assuring travel up the correct gully. (Visually locate the spire and gully before leaving Split Rock.)

Travel up the gully along the left side until travel looks easier on the right side. Cross to the right side of the gully and travel to the ridgetop behind a large pine tree. Drop down the other side of the ridge a short distance to a hollow. Continue up the opposite side of the hollow to another ridgetop — about 100 yards ENE of the spire. Travel down the other side of this ridge about 25 yards. Locate a pile of white mine tailings and a horizontal mine shaft about ten feet deep. From the tailings pile, travel NNE. Pass to the right of the nearby large boulder and to the left of the three leaning slabs. Follow a trail (about 40 yards) to the top of a ridge. Drop down the other side of the ridge and continue about 50' to a sharp bend in the trail. From here, leave the main trail and head north on an obscure trail to reach a small, relatively open plateau. There is a mine concealed beneath an oak tree near the center of the plateau. The house within the boulders is on the east side of the plateau. Find another rock shelter (less preserved) and fireplace by traveling 100' up the passageway located outside the window side of the house.

(Respect hikers that follow who would like to see the ruins in their present state; don't disturb any of the ruins.)

8. SPLIT ROCK LOOP

New Hike

Type: trail, day
Mileage: 2.4 miles (round-trip)
Time: 1-2 hours
Difficulty: easy
Elevation Extremes: 4220'- 4350'   **Difference:** 130'
Starting and Ending Point: Split Rock Picnic Area (4280')
Topo Maps: Queen Mtn. 7.5'   **Appendix D Map:** # 4

Summary: Split Rock Loop is one of several newly designated park trails. It winds through a boulder maze and leads to some interesting rock formations known as "The Tooth", "Tulip Rock", and "Face Rock" (pictured left). Traveling counterclockwise, the first part of the loop leads through thick stands of yucca plants as it weaves around isolated rock mounds. The latter part of the loop travels more deeply into the maze, through large steep-faced boulder piles.

Route: The trail starts at Split Rock, a massive boulder that is split in two. From the parking lot, walk around the left side of Split Rock to a cave on the rock's north side. The cave is formed by the overhanging edges of the giant boulder. The trail heads north from the cave.

At 0.3 miles, there is a junction for the Eagle Cliff Hike. (See preceding hike.) Take a sharp left at this junction and follow the trail southwest. After hiking about one mile, start looking for Tulip Rock. This towering formation is only a short distance from the trail. It's easy to miss this formation while hiking the loop in a counterclockwise direction; be sure to look behind and to the right of the trail. To the west of Tulip Rock is a large bulbous rock that looks like a molar — The Tooth.

Around mile 1.3, the trail enters a wash where a sign identifies a junction. From this junction, a short side trip leads through a wash to Face Rock. This rock somewhat resembles the profile of President George Washington.

To reach Face Rock, turn right at the junction and travel down the wash about 300 yards. The wash leads past an old watering trough and continues to a rock wall where it becomes choked between the wall and a large juniper tree. The rock wall is Face Rock; however, the face is easier to see before reaching the wall. To continue the loop trail, backtrack up the wash to the junction and follow the trail northeast.

A hiker gives size perspective to Tulip Rock.

About 1/4 mile beyond the junction, the trail makes a sharp bend to the left. This is an area of possible confusion since a small drainage continues from this point in an eastern direction. Follow the trail to the northwest. Just past this bend, look for another viewpoint of Tulip Rock off the left (northwest) side of the trail. The formation stands alone and is easy to recognize.

Continue following the trail to a small wash. Turn right and travel down the wash a short way to a larger wash. Follow this wash to the left. Look for a large cairn sitting on a boulder to the north; it marks the general area of the trail. The trail ends at the south side of the parking area.

Note: The National Park Service may expand this trail in the future.

9. SKULL ROCK - (See Chapter 5, Hike # 8.)

10. CROWN PRINCE LOOKOUT (4581')

Type: road-trail / x-country, day
Mileage: 3 miles (round-trip)
Time: 2 hours
Difficulty: moderate with short section of scrambling
Elevation Extremes: 4400'- 4581'   **Difference:** 181'
Starting and Ending Point: Jumbo Rocks Campground Entrance (4400')
Topo Maps: Malapai Hill 7.5'   **Appendix D Map:** # 8

Summary: An easy hike followed by a short scramble leads to a hilltop where a lookout tower was once perched. The lookout was an airplane warning station possibly built during World War II. Today nothing remains of the lookout except a 3'x3' cement block and some anchor points. The summit of this hill offers an excellent 360° view.

Route: From Jumbo Rocks Entrance, walk west along Park Boulevard about 1/4 mile. Find the road-trail that leaves from the south side of Park Boulevard. Large rocks separate the road-trail from the paved road. The National Park Service has tried to naturalize the beginning of this road-trail by transplanting native vegetation. Walk to the side of the road-trail to avoid disturbing the transplant area.

Follow this road-trail approximately 3/4 mile to a fork. Turn right at the fork and continue traveling on the road-trail until it ends at the base of a rocky hill. From here follow an obscure trail along the northeast side of the hill to a steep rocky area. A short scramble up (ten vertical feet) the rocks leads to a more obvious trail. Continue following the trail to the flat, open area on the summit. (Note: The Crown Prince road-trail is pictured but not labeled on the USGS topographical map.)

Chapter 7
PARK BOULEVARD WEST

The western half of Park Boulevard travels through a variety of terrain as it leads from the West Entrance to Sheep Pass. Hikes originating from this road travel to the top of high peaks, into the rugged Wonderland, up wild and lush canyons, and down quiet sandy washes that gently wind through Joshua tree forests. Campgrounds along this section of road include Hidden Valley and Ryan campgrounds and Sheep Pass Group Campground. A backcountry board is located at the Boy Scout Trailhead, a couple miles west of Hidden Valley Picnic Area.

1. BURRO LOOP

New Hike

Type: trail,day
Mileage: 7.2 miles (round-trip)
Time: 4 - 5 hours
Difficulty: moderately strenuous
Elevation Extremes: 3020' - 3560'   **Difference:** 540'
Starting and Ending Point: West Entrance (3520')
Topo Maps: Joshua Tree South 7.5', Indian Cove 7.5'

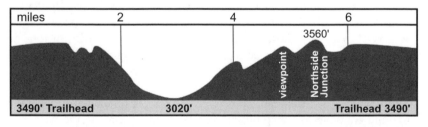

Summary: In the 1990's, this corner of the park was the hangout for a lone burro that roamed the drainages and rocky hills. Nobody knows for sure how the burro got there, but the assumption is that he was part of the BLM Burro Adoption Program. He either escaped from, or was released by, his adoptive owner. During the burro's reign over the area, trails were numer-

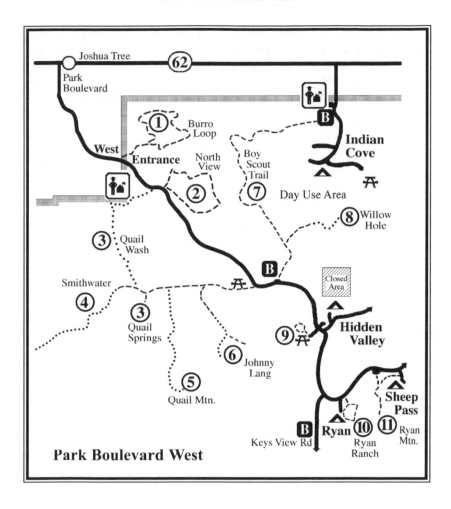

ous. It was amazing to see the amount of resource impact made by one out-of-place animal. Today the numerous trails have faded and the fate of the burro is unknown.

This hike travels through what was once the burro's playground. It winds through large rocky hills, boulder piles, and canyons. High points offer views of Mt. San Gorgonio to the west and the sprawling desert communities to the north.

The park's recently approved backcountry plan established this as a new park trail. Although the trail crew has worked on and defined the trail, they have yet to install any signs. Without signs, the trail can be confusing in wash areas. Hikers should be prepared to use map and compass skills to navigate the loop successfully.

51

Route: This route description provides detailed directions for navigating an unmarked route. Once the trail is marked, these details may be unnecessary.

Locate the trailhead at the northwest corner of the block wall at the park boundary. Before leaving the trailhead, note the lone rocky hill located NNE from the trailhead. This landmark will help prevent confusion created by intersecting horse social trails. The trail travels to the base of the hill then veers to the right (east) side of the hill.

About 0.2 miles from the trailhead, there is an obvious fork in the trail. Take the left fork that heads north toward the hill landmark. The trail branches into the loop portion of the hike 1.1 miles from the trailhead. This hike is described for clockwise travel; take the left fork.

Follow the trail down into a wash then up a drainage into the rocky hills. The trail leads up and down over ridges then enters a large wash at mile 2.2. (The trail that continues on the other side of the wash is an alternative access. See Onaga Option below.)

Burro Loop Trail / USGS Indian Cove 7.5', Joshua Tree South 7.5'

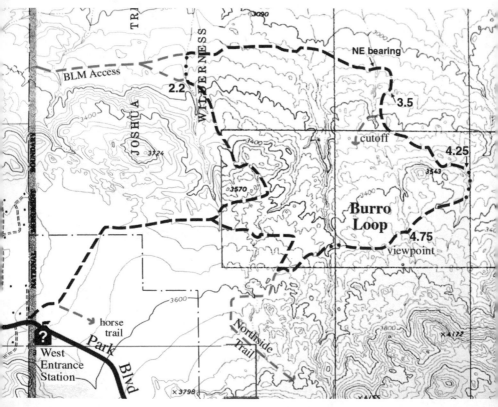

Turn right and head north down the wash 250 yards. At a point where the wash significantly widens, look to the right to find the trail leading up out of the wash. This next section of the trail travels over more gentle, open terrain. Travel 1/2 mile to a wash; find the continuing trail straight across. Hike 0.3 miles to another wash. The trail continues almost straight across the wash, but it is difficult to see. Follow a compass bearing of NE across the wash to make it easier to find the trail.

The trail begins to head south up through a rocky corridor. Watch for a fork in the drainage (mile 3.5) where the trail bends to the right. The trail leads up another rocky corridor, travels around a corner, then ascends the left bank of the drainage. At mile 3.7, the trail tops out on a ridge. Here there is a trail fork that may be difficult to recognize. The right fork leads down into a gully then up through a red dirt gorge. This trail is a planned short-cut that will provide an option of shortening the loop by a half mile. Currently however, the short-cut trail is not well defined. Take the left fork, which leads south up into the rock piles.

The trail travels through a maze of rocky hills, boulders, and canyons. At mile 4.25, the trail enters a small wash. Head south (right) up the wash about 250 yards to a bend in the drainage. (Note: The trail leaves the wash in two places for horses to skirt boulder obstructions.) The trail leads southwest out of the wash over gentler, open terrain. Enter a wash at mile 4.75; the trail continues a few feet down the wash to the right.

Climb the trail to a ridgetop then descend a drainage to a major wash. The trail enters the wash at a horseshoe bend. Go up the wash about 50 yards to find the continuing trail on the west side of the wash. Travel 0.3 miles and look carefully for a trail junction; it is not well defined. At this intersection, the obvious trail bends to the south. This is the Northside Trail, an unimproved access trail. The less obvious Burro Loop bends to the north.

Follow the trail north 0.2 miles to a sharp bend. Again watch carefully; two faint social trails (one coming from the north and one from the east) intersect at this point. Follow the Burro Loop as it makes a sharp bend to the west and travel 250 yards to a wash. Go left up the wash about 45 yards to find the trail that exits to the right. The faint trail winds a short way up a ridge to a more defined trail above. Hike the last 0.2 miles back to the beginning of the loop near the rocky hill landmark. Turn left onto the access trail and travel back to the trailhead.

Onaga Option: The park's trail crew has improved a half-mile access trail that leads from the loop to the park's west boundary. This area can be accessed by driving east on Onaga Trail. A rough dirt road leads into a primitive day use area administered by the town of Joshua Tree. Most cars can travel the road for about 1.9 miles. Travel the remaining 0.7 miles on foot to reach the trail at the park boundary.

2. NORTH VIEW / MAZE / WINDOW ROCK LOOP

New Hike

Type: trail, day/overnight
Mileage: 6.6 mile loop
Time: 4 - 6 hours
Difficulty: moderately strenuous
Elevation Extremes: 3950' - 4340'   **Difference:** 390'
Starting and Ending Point: Borrow Pit Parking Area (3960')
Topo Maps: Indian Cove 7.5'

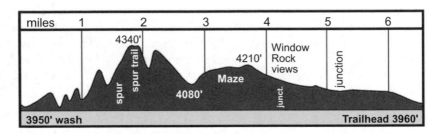

Summary: This newly designated trail has much to offer. It leads to high vistas and travels past an odd shaped window located high up on a rocky hill. The trail covers varied terrain including rolling hills, steep mountainsides, high ridgetops, sheltered ravines, wide desert washes, and gentle open areas. For a short section, the trail winds through an area of boulders known as the Maze.

Vegetation is equally varied with large nolinas, yuccas, junipers, pines, cacti, and of course, Joshua trees. Under the right spring conditions, beautiful blue Canterberry bell flowers are abundant.

Route: From the parking lot, walk up a dirt roadway about 40 yards. Head left on the trail that crosses the road. Travel 75 yards and take a sharp right at a fork in the trail. Follow the trail to the northeast side of a gravel pit then into a wash. As the gravel pit disappears behind a low ridge, the trail forks again. Take the left fork. The trail that continues straight up the wash is the Maze Loop cutoff (see options below). Note: When the new parking lot is created at the trailhead, the trail start will change. New signs should prevent confusion.

From this junction, the trail begins winding up through rolling rocky hills that sit between larger boulder-covered mountains. The trail climbs repeatedly up and down from ridgetops to ravines.

At mile 1.6, a short spur trail (0.2 miles) leads to a precipice boasting broad views of the desert towns and mountains located north of the park. About 1/4 mile farther along the main trail, a shorter spur leads to another

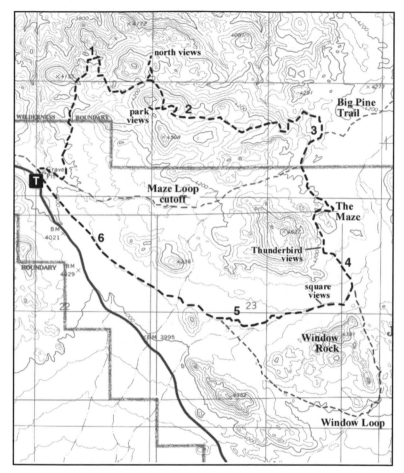

North View Trail System / USGS Indian Cove 7.5'

ridgetop view. From here, there are excellent views of the park interior—over to Park Boulevard and beyond to Quail Mountain, the highest mountain in the park. (Look below for the miniaturized cars at the trailhead to gain an increased sense of accomplishment for your ascent efforts.)

From the second spur, the trail follows a ridge and begins a gradual descent into a drainage. A final short steep section brings the trail into a small wash. Travel down this wash a short distance to intersect a larger wash. Turn right, go sixty yards, then take the left fork. Follow the trail markers through this potentially confusing area of washes and drainages. The trail will become more visible shortly.

At mile 3, there is another trail junction. The left fork is the Big Pine Trail; it leads over to the Boy Scout Trail (see options below). Take the southern trail (right fork) to continue the loop. Within 1/4 mile, the trail passes the Maze Loop cutoff. Continue to the left at this fork.

The trail soon enters the Maze at the base of a large boulder-covered mountain. Wind through the narrow passages that lead through piles of low boulder mounds. In this section, there are several beautiful large nolina plants near the trail.

As the trail leaves the Maze and heads out into the open, Window Rock becomes visible. These early views of Window Rock are the most striking. On top of the most prominent rocky peak to the south appears an opening in the shape of a thunderbird (an upright side profile of a bird with its huge wings outstretched). Later, as the trail continues past the front of this peak, the window transforms into an ordinary square.

At mile 4.3, the trail enters a wash. (Continuing across the wash leads to a southern loop trail around Window Rock—see options below.) At this junction, turn right (west) and head down the wash in front of Window Rock. In about 1/2 mile, the trail exits the wash and begins a gradual turn back to the north. At mile 5.2, the trail passes the second junction with the southern loop. Head northwest (right). From here back to the parking area, the trail travels over fairly level terrain forested with Joshua trees.

See topographical map on page 50.

Hike Options

Maze Loop: This trail bypasses the rocky hills to the north. It shortens the loop by 1.75 miles; however, it misses much of the interesting terrain and views for which this hike is noted.

Big Pine Trail: This 1.8 mile trail leads to the mid point of the Boy Scout Trail (see Hike # 6). A 0.6 mile spur leads north from the Big Pine Trail to a large pine tree with a diameter of about 3'. This lone pine is unusually large for a desert pine. Other natural features that deserve mentioning are large groups of barrel cacti and a quartz outcropping. The barrel cacti border the trail about one mile from the North View/Big Pine trail junction. About 1/2 mile farther, the trail travels over a hill paved with large chunks of white quartz.

Window Loop: Taking this southern trail extension adds one mile to the hike. The trail leads around the base of the Window Rock peak through pleasant terrain and vegetation. The views of Window Rock are limited on this section.

3. QUAIL SPRINGS ROAD-TRAIL / WASH

Type: road-trail/cross-country, day/overnight
Mileage: 7.8 miles to Quail Springs (round trip)
         8.5 miles to West Entrance Wash (one-way)
Time: 4 - 5 hours
Difficulty: easy
Elevation Extremes: 3350' - 3979'   **Difference:** 629'
Starting Point: Quail Springs Picnic Area (3979')
Ending Point: Quail Springs Picnic Area (3979') / West Entrance Wash (3800')
Topo Maps: Indian Cove 7.5', Joshua Tree South 7.5'   **Appendix D Map:** # 6

Summary: This route travels across an open valley dotted with Joshua trees, passes through a mountain gap into a large isolated basin, then follows a wash through the basin to the north boundary. At the mouth of Smith Water Canyon, look for a concentrated stand of Joshua trees. This is a picturesque place to camp.

To find Quail Springs locate a large rock cistern near the mountain gap. The cistern, a historical holding tank for water, is now dry. Water can usually be found trickling from the spring on the hillside above the tank. During the wetter months, a small, lush green oasis flourishes around the spring. (Don't depend on finding water at the spring for drinking.)

There is an interesting side trip not far from Quail Springs. The route leads to a collection of engraved rock slabs. A Swedish immigrant, who homesteaded the area in the early 1900's, carved his philosophical beliefs on the rocks. Ask a ranger for more information on the area. (Vandalism is a major concern for these unique, irreplaceable carvings.)

Route: Travel west on the road-trail that leaves from the western corner of the back parking lot. Watch for the point where the road-trail exits the wash on the south side, about 3/4 mile from the picnic area. (The road-trail provides easier traveling; the wash eventually heads in a different direction.) Follow the road-trail and intermittent wash until they pass through the remains of a fence. Just beyond the fence, the wash bends sharply to the right. At this point, the road-trail leaves the wash on the left side and continues straight. The road-trail, which is somewhat obscure, travels SW toward the base of the southern hills.

To reach Quail Springs follow the road-trail as it bends to the south. If finding the road-trail is too difficult, travel x/country west along the base of the southern mountains. Head south up through a section of fire-blackened Joshua trees to the base of a rocky cirque. The cistern and spring are along the western edge of this cirque.

To continue to the north boundary, backtrack to the point where the road-trail turned south. Continue a short distance farther to access the main wash. Follow the wash northwest into the large sloping basin. (An inter-mittent jeep trail parallels the wash, but it is difficult to follow.) Just be-fore the boundary, the wash enters a canyon. A barbed wire fence spans the wash at this point. Continue past this fence about 1/4 mile to reach a boul-der and cable fence marked with National Park Service boundary signs.

Travel right (east) along the fence toward the hills. Locate and follow the faint road-trail that parallels the fence on the south side. Continue fol-lowing the road-trail east up into a side wash (West Entrance Wash). Follow the wash up through the canyon. About 1.25 miles from the fence, there is a perpendicular fork in the wash. Take the left fork and follow it 1/4 mile to Park Boulevard.

4. SMITH WATER CANYON - (See Chapter 13, Hike # 13.)

5. QUAIL MOUNTAIN (5813')

Type: road-trail/x-country, day/overnight
Mileage: 12 miles (round-trip)
Time: 7 - 9 hours
Difficulty: strenuous, difficult
Elevation Extremes: 3680' - 5813'   **Difference:** 2133'
Starting and Ending Point: Quail Springs Picnic Area (3979')
Topo Maps: Indian Cove 7.5', Joshua Tree South 7.5'   **Appendix D Map:** # 6

Summary: This beautiful hike leads up an unlikely verdant canyon to the summit of the park's highest peak. The narrow canyon contains thick grasses, rushes, and trees growing among water-streaked rocks and clear pools (seasonal). It is in surprising contrast to the surrounding dry desert and stark, fire-blackened summit of Quail Mountain. The lush canyon is susceptible to impact; make overnight camps only at the dryer base of the canyon or on the broad summit.

As can be expected, there is an excellent 360° view from the summit. Look for the climbing register near the large cairn that marks the summit. (Note: This is a confusing route. It is easy to get off-track and end up on one of the surrounding peaks. See Chapter 10 for an easier route to the summit.) (Postnote 2001: Quail Mountain burned again in the 1999 wildfires.)

Route: Follow Quail Springs Road-Trail approximately three miles. (See Hike # 3.) Head south up the second wide valley. (The first canyon is Johnny Lang Canyon.) This valley funnels into a narrow canyon. Quail Mountain is the broad rounded mountain centered above this valley and canyon. Follow the main wash up through the narrow canyon. The canyon forks several times; stay in the large, main wash. When a fork in the canyon results in two washes of apparently equal size, take the left wash.

Travel becomes more difficult in the upper reaches of the canyon. There are some short sections of difficult boulder scrambling and low-angle slab climbing (class III). The wash forks again at a higher, fire-scarred, more open section of the mountain. Take the left fork and follow the wash to an open, flat area. The summit is up to the east. (Note: The high peaks surrounding Quail are pointed — in contrast to Quail's large, rounded, almost flat summit. This fact should help eliminate some confusion.)

6. JOHNNY LANG CANYON / MINE / VIEWPOINT

Type: road-trail/x-country, day/overnight
Mileage: 10.5 miles to end of canyon (round-trip)
  9 miles to mine (round-trip)
  7.5 miles to viewpoint (round-trip)
Time: 6 - 7 hours
Difficulty: canyon — moderate, moderately difficult
    (mine — strenuous, viewpoint — moderately strenuous)
Elevation Extremes: 3979' - 4400' (mine — 4800', viewpoint — 4380')
Difference: 421' (821', 401')
Starting and Ending Point: Quail Springs Picnic Area (3979')
Topo Maps: Indian Cove 7.5'   **Appendix D Map:** # 6

Summary: This hike offers a variety of terrain, vegetation, and views. Johnny Lang Canyon is named after the early prospector who began the Lost Horse Mine operations. After Johnny sold his shares in the Lost Horse Mine, he moved into a small cabin in this canyon. He worked his mining claim in the hills above his little house. The scanty remains of his cabin are near the mouth of the canyon. The mine shafts remain as Johnny left them. (Mines are unstable and dangerous; maintain a safe distance from their openings. Refer to Chapter 3, "Hazards - Use Caution.")

Quiet beauty was probably an important aspect that drew Lang to this particular canyon. It is still an isolated and beautiful place. Many large pinyon pines grow in the rugged, rocky valley of the upper canyon. Small pools of water can sometimes be found in the sandy and rocky washes. At the cabin site, near the mouth of the canyon, clear water (seasonal and intermittent) flows down the rocky wash. From the mine and approach ridges, there are good views of the Wonderland of Rocks and the surrounding valley.

A scenic side trip from the cabin site leads up (300' in elevation) along the east side of the canyon. This old prospector trail steadily and rapidly climbs to a high vantage point. The route passes an impressive collection of

59

pancake and barrel cacti high up on the rocky slopes. Johnny Lang probably used this trail to reach mines on the other side of the mountain.

Route: Travel about two miles west on the road-trail that leaves from the western corner of the back parking lot. (Watch for the point where the road-trail exits the wash on the south side, about 3/4 mile from the picnic area.) Turn south on a road-trail that leads up the first large valley. From here, either travel up the wash or along the road-trail. (The road-trail becomes faint and difficult to follow in spots.)

The meager remains of Johnny's cabin are at the end of this road-trail. Look for the ruins just before the point where the wash enters the narrowed canyon. The ruins are located above and 50' to the right (west) of the wash.

Continue up the rocky wash to attain the upper valley. A short section of difficult scrambling leads to the uppermost part of the valley. Avoid this difficult section by leaving the right side of the wash (just before the difficult section) and traveling up between two rocky knolls. Climbing over the ridge at the southern end of Johnny Lang Canyon will lead to Lost Horse Valley (Note: There are private properties near this section of Lost Horse Valley. Respect the landowners' rights; do not trespass.)

Johnny Lang Mine: To reach the mine, continue 1/2 mile up the wash from the cabin site. Climb a knoll on the south (right) side of the wash. The mining trail that ascends the knoll is barely visible. (This knoll can be identified when the canyon opens and a distant, high rounded mountain — set back from the right side of the wash — becomes visible. The knoll is close to the wash and left of this mountain.) From the top of the knoll, look south across a side canyon to locate the mine tailings amidst a thick section of pine and oak trees. A mining trail that leads up to the mine is also visible at this point.

Viewpoint: From the cabin site, look across the wash and up the hillside. There is a large rock cairn located on the hillside (at 95°) about 250 yards away. (The cairn, which blends in with the rocky hillside, is difficult to spot.) The cairn marks the prospector trail. From the cairn, follow the faint, narrow, rocky trail southeast up the mountainside. The trail disappears at the saddle on the south side of the mountain. (Note: This trail is not maintained; use caution while travelling across the steep slopes.)

7. BOY SCOUT TRAIL

Type: trail, day/overnight
Mileage: 8 miles (one-way)
Time: 4 - 5 hours
Difficulty: moderate (travel south to north)
Elevation Extremes: 2840' - 4185'   **Difference:** 1345'
Starting Point: Boy Scout Trailhead (4040')
Ending Point: Indian Cove Backcountry Board (2840')
Topo Maps: Indian Cove 7.5'   **Appendix D Map:** # 7

Summary: The Boy Scout Trail provides a variety of terrain and views. It is fairly easy to follow and travels mostly downhill to Indian Cove. The first portion of the trail leads along the edge of the Wonderland of Rocks. It follows picturesque, sandy washes lined with junipers, pinyon pines, and oak trees. The latter portion of the trail travels along a rocky mountainside, winds through steep mountains and narrow canyons, and then continues through the open desert to Indian Cove. There are many pleasant places for camping not far from the trail. Small backpacking parties will enjoy camping near sandy washes shaded by the large trees and rocks — approximately 3.5 miles from the trailhead. (Note: Camping is only allowed on the west side of the trail. The east side of the trail is day use only. Be aware of flash flood danger when camping near washes.)

Route: Follow the trail 1.4 miles north from the parking area to a fork. Take the trail to the left. (The right fork leads to a wash that descends into Willow Hole. See Chapter 16, Hike #3.) About four miles from the parking lot, the trail makes a sharp left turn out of a wash. This turn may be poorly identified. Missing the turn will result in travel into a steep, nearly impassable canyon. To prevent this error, watch for a tank and water trough in the wash.

A tank is a barrier that spans the width of a wash. Pioneers used tanks during the ranching days to collect water for cattle. They built this particular tank by cementing small walls of rock on the sides of a natural boulder obstruction. The tank is filled with sand and no longer holds water.

About 300 yards beyond the tank and trough, the trail leaves the wash and heads west (left). The remainder of the trail should pose no problem. (Note: This trail is pictured on topographical maps. However, both the first mile and the last mile of the trail have been rerouted since the topographical maps were printed.) This trail is also commonly hiked from Indian Cove uphill to the Boy Scout Trailhead.

8. WILLOW HOLE / WONDERLAND
(See Chapter 16, Hike # 3.)

61

9. HIDDEN VALLEY NATURE TRAIL
(See Chapter 5, Hike # 4.)

10. RYAN RANCH HOMESTEAD

New Hike

Type: trail/road-trail, day
Mileage: 1 mile loop
Time: 1 hour
Difficulty: easy
Elevation Extremes: relatively level
Starting and Ending Point: Ryan Campground, small parking lot on southeast corner of loop road (4340')
Topo Maps: Keys View 7.5'   **Appendix D Map:** # 9

Summary: Not far from Ryan Campground, lie the remains of an old ranch. This homestead belonged to the Ryan brothers, Jep and Thomas, two of the Lost Horse Mine owners (See Chapter 10, Hike # 6). The brothers established the homestead to gain a reliable water source for their mining operations.

The most interesting remains at the homestead are the red adobe ruins. The largest ruin was a three-room ranch house built around 1900. It burnt in 1978, but the outer walls still stand. Look out the window openings and enjoy the view from the house. It is no wonder the Ryans picked this site for the house.

Near the ranch, there is an old cemetery with about eight graves. Rings of rocks, which have become hidden by vegetation, are the only markers for most of the grave sites. A couple of the graves have dates, ranging from 1893–1897, painted on nearby boulders. Judging from the size of the rock circles, at least one of the graves might have belonged to an infant.

Route: For easier trail finding, clockwise travel is recommended. The trail travels through Joshua trees and small boulder piles as it leads a short distance to the edge of Headstone Rock. This large overhanging boulder block provides a dramatic route for rock climbers.

At mile 0.2, the trail intersects the old road that leads to the ranch house. Turn right and follow the road 0.1 miles. There are two boulder piles along the right side of the road. Look for the cemetery near the smaller of the two piles. Just past the cemetery, there is a cultural site sign. At this point, the driveway to the ranch house departs the left side of the road. Just beyond the sign, the loop trail leaves the right side of the road and follows a remnant jeep trail.

As a side trip, it is worth following the road an extra 1/4 mile. The road leads past another small adobe ruin, the remains of a windmill, and a well house. It continues uphill to a good viewpoint located on the south side of a large boulder cluster.

The loop trail continues south from the homestead to intersect the California Riding and Hiking Trail. Turn right at this junction and follow the trail back to the parking lot.

This hike can also be accessed from Ryan Ranch Parking Area on Park Boulevard. A 0.4 mile road-trail leaves the parking area and intersects the north corner of the loop trail near Headstone Rock.

11. RYAN MOUNTAIN (5457')

Type: trail, day
Mileage: 3 miles (round-trip)
Time: 2 - 3 hours
Difficulty: moderately strenuous
Elevation Extremes: 4390' - 5457'   **Difference:** 1067'
Starting and Ending Point: Ryan Mountain Parking Area (4390')
Topo Maps: Keys View 7.5', Indian Cove 7.5'   **Appendix D Map:** # 9

Summary: The Ryan Mountain trail and summit provide some of the best panoramic views in the park. The 360° view from the summit includes Mt. San Jacinto, Mt. San Gorgonio, most of the park valleys, Pinto Basin, the Wonderland of Rocks, and more. The trail travels continuously uphill. There are several sections of stone steps constructed from rocks found in the area.

While traveling up the trail, look west to the rock formation known as Saddle Rocks and watch for rock climbers. The longest technical climbing routes in the park are on this formation.

Alternative Start: A spur trail leaves from Sheep Pass Campground, from both Site #1 and across the road from Site #6. Leaving from Sheep Pass adds 1.5 miles round-trip. The spur trail joins the main trail about 0.2 miles from the Ryan Mountain Parking Area.

Mt. San Jacinto and Lost Horse Valley from Ryan Mountain

Chapter 8
QUEEN VALLEY

Queen Valley contains one of the larger Joshua tree forests in the park. The valley is bounded by mountains to the north and Pleasant Valley to the south. A system of dirt roads travels through the center of Queen Valley. These roads are a starting point for several hikes to areas of both natural and historical interest. The dirt roads can be accessed at three locations — a dirt road near Barker Dam Parking Lot; a northwest-bound road that leaves Park Boulevard east of Sheep Pass; and a road leading north off Park Boulevard 1.6 miles west of Jumbo Rocks Campground. The Pine City Backcountry Board is in the northeast corner of this road system.

1. BIG BARKER DAM LOOP

Type: trail/road-trail, day
Mileage: 3 mile loop
Time: 2 hours
Difficulty: easy, easy scrambling
Elevation Extremes: fairly level
Starting and Ending Point: Barker Dam Parking Area (4250')
Topo Maps: Indian Cove 7.5'   **Appendix D Map:** # 7

Summary: This hike is an extension of the Barker Dam Nature Trail. The route travels past the exhibits and historical sites on the nature trail. Then it branches off, adding distance and a variety of terrain and scenery.

The route leaves the nature trail and winds through large rock formations. Watch for rock climbers along the way. This area is one of the most popular climbing areas in the park. The return leg of the loop climbs a short rocky section before rejoining the nature trail. For a complete description of the Barker Dam area, refer to Chapter 5, Hike # 5.

Route: Follow the nature trail north to the dam. From the base of the dam, follow the trail about 1/4 mile to a junction. At this point, a directional arrow indicates an abrupt left turn. However, don't turn left. Instead, trav-

QUEEN VALLEY

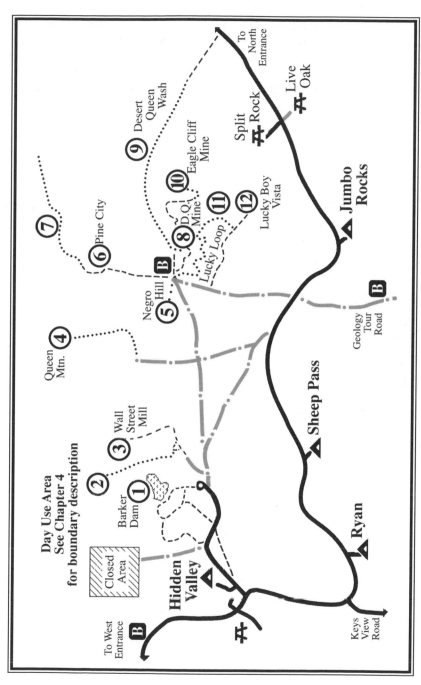

Queen Valley

65

el down the road-trail that leads west. Travel 0.2 miles and turn left at a fork. Continue about 0.3 miles to the next fork and turn right. Follow the trail out to a dirt road, turn left, and travel a short way to Echo Intersection.

Turn left and walk about 0.2 miles along the paved road to a pullout. The trail crosses the road just east of the pullout. (Traveling south on the trail leads to Hidden Valley Campground.) Head north (left) on the trail. The trail leads to a wash, crosses the wash, then continues to a rocky gully. Watch for posts marking this section of the trail. Climb up through the gully to reach the continuing trail, which leads to the petroglyph rock. Continue 100 feet beyond the petroglyphs and head east (right) at the junction. Follow the trail back to the Barker Dam Parking Lot.

2. WONDERLAND RANCH WASH

(See Chapter 16, Hike # 2.)

3. WALL STREET MILL

Type: road-trail, day
Mileage: 1.5 miles (round-trip)
Time: 1 hour
Difficulty: easy
Elevation Extremes: 4280' - 4340'   **Difference:** 60'
Starting and Ending Point: Wonderland Ranch Parking Area   (4280')
Topo Maps: Indian Cove 7.5'   **Appendix D Map:** # 7

Summary: Bill Keys owned the Wall Street Mill. He used the mill to process ore from the Desert Queen Mine. Wall Street is not the largest mill in the park, but it is well preserved. It is an important part of the park's history.

Look for a stone marker on the way to the mill. The stone reads, "Here is Where Worth Bagly Bit the dust At the HAND of W.F. KEYS, May 11, 1943." Bagley was killed in a shoot-out with Keys in a controversy over the use of the road. After spending five years in prison, Keys was found not-guilty. The courts ruled that Keys shot in self-defense.

Surrounding the mill, there are several old cars, trucks, and pieces of machinery — more reminders of the early mining days. The mill lies in a picturesque area on the edge of the Wonderland. Traveling in the wash past the mill leads to a rocky maze vegetated with oak, manzanita, and jojoba.

Route: From the parking area, follow the road-trail about 50 yards to a fork. From here, either take the left (NW) fork toward the remains of a pink ranch house, or bypass the house by continuing NE (right fork) on a less-traveled road-trail. (A short distance farther, the two road-trails join back together. There is an old model truck located just NW of the point where the two trails rejoin.) The road-trail continues to a windmill and the Desert Queen Well. It bends to the east around the windmill, passes through the remains of a barbed-wire fence, then makes a hairpin turn. The "shoot-out" stone is on the left side of the road-trail past the hairpin turn. The road-trail eventually narrows to the size of a path. At this point, begin looking to the left (west) for the mill.

4. QUEEN MOUNTAIN (5687')

Type: x-country, day/overnight (note day use area)
Mileage: 4 miles (round-trip)
Time: 3 - 4 hours
Difficulty: strenuous, moderately difficult
Elevation Extremes: 4480' - 5687'   **Difference:** 1207'
Starting and Ending Point: O'Dell Parking Area (4480')
Topo Maps: Queen Mtn. 7.5'   **Appendix D Map:** # 7 & 8

Summary: Queen Mountain is the most prominent peak in Queen Valley. A short hike through a wash, followed by a rugged climb up a trail-less mountainside, leads to good views of the Wonderland of Rocks, Queen and Lost Horse valleys, and distant Mt. San Gorgonio. Desert bighorn sheep are occasionally seen on the slopes of Queen Mountain or on the rocky peaks directly to the north. Golden eagles can sometimes be seen flying near the cliffs on these mountains.

A rugged climb up a gully (center of picture) leads to the summit of Queen Mountain — the pointed peak pictured left center.

Queen Mountain is within a day use area. However, camping is allowed near the south base of the mountain outside the restricted area. Overnight users need to start from the Pine City Backcountry Board; this will make the trip longer and less direct. There is a climbing register on the summit.

Route: From O'Dell Parking Area, head east (< 1/4 mile) to the second sandy wash. Travel up the wash, which heads generally northeast. Follow the wash through some low hills and on to the base of the mountain near an obvious slide area. Continue following the wash (now rocky) up a steep rocky grade. Follow the wash as it makes a sharp turn to the west. (Rocky cliffs stretch across the mountain above this point.) A hundred yards farther, the route departs from the wash (as marked on the topographical maps). It continues NNW up an obvious route — a rocky gully with steep sides. The gully opens up near the summit. Climb up along the right side of the gully (near the base of the cliffs). Continue to the ridge between the two high summits — 5687' and 5677'. From the ridge, head west to the higher of the two points. A large slab leads to the summit. Look for the climbing register in a pile of rocks under a large dead tree limb.

5. NEGRO HILL (4875')

Type: x-country, day
Mileage: 1.5 miles (round-trip)
Time: 1.5 hours
Difficulty: moderately strenuous
Elevation Extremes: 4436' - 4875'   **Difference:** 439'
Starting and Ending Point: Pine City Backcountry Board (4436')
Topo Maps: Queen Mtn. 7.5'   **Appendix D Map:** # 4

Summary: A seemingly unremarkable hill stands alone on the eastern edge of Queen Valley. Negro Hill, may look uninteresting from the base; however, the short hike to the summit is well worth the effort. The 360° view from the summit includes Mt. San Jacinto, Mt. San Gorgonio, Queen Valley, Quail Mountain, Pine City, Eagle Cliff Hills, the Wonderland, distant mountain ranges to the south and east, and more. The open summit provides a good vantage point for enjoying the colorful desert sunsets. (Use care when descending the hill in low light; there is no trail and the ground is rocky.)

Route: Negro Hill is the obvious hill located a short distance west of the backcountry board. Head west up any likely slope.

6. PINE CITY

Type: trail, day/overnight (note day use area)
Mileage: 3 miles (round-trip)
Time: 2 hours
Difficulty: easy
Elevation Extremes: 4436' - 4563'   **Difference:** 127'
Starting and Ending Point: Pine City Backcountry Board (4436')
Topo Maps: Queen Mtn. 7.5'   **Appendix D Map:** # 4 & 8

Summary: It takes less than an hour to hike to Pine City, but it can take more than a day to explore and enjoy the quiet solitude of this pretty area. The area was not a city or town. At most, there were one or two small cabins which are now gone. A few collapsed mine shafts are the only remains of this small mining area.

However, it is the island of desert greenery, and not the history, that draws hikers to this area. Large pine trees grow among an isolated collection of rocky walls and boulder mounds. This is an excellent place for bird watching. Bighorn sheep are known to inhabit the area, particularly in the summer months. Most of Pine City lies just inside the day use area, but camping is allowed on the southern edge of the area.

Route: The trail leaves the northwest side of the parking lot. A spur trail branches off to the right (east), 0.5 miles from the parking lot. This rocky, overgrown trail leads to a ridge and the remains of a mining camp. At this same junction, a rough trail leads left (west) through Queen Valley. Continue on the main trail to reach Pine City. (The other trails marked on the topographical map are overgrown and difficult or impossible to follow.)

Upon reaching the Pine City boulder area, the trail travels to the west around the boulders and up to an overlook of a deep ravine. The mine shafts are along this section of the trail. (Mine shafts are dangerous; maintain a safe distance from their openings. Refer to Chapter 3, "Hazards - Use Caution.")

7. PINE CITY CANYON

Type: road-trail/x-country, day/overnight (note day use area)
Mileage: 5.5 miles (one-way)
Time: 4 hours
Difficulty: moderate, difficult
Elevation Extremes: 2920' - 4580'   **Difference:** 1660'
Starting Point: Pine City Backcountry Board (4436')
Ending Point: North Entrance Exhibit (2920')
Topo Maps: Queen Mtn. 7.5'   **Appendix D Map:** # 8

Summary: A hike down Pine City Canyon provides an adventuresome addition to the Pine City hike (Hike # 6). This hike affords the opportunity to
enjoy both the gentle quiet of Pine City and some interesting boulder scrambling in the canyon. After leaving Pine City, the route follows a wash down
through a narrow, steep-sided canyon. Easy wash walking is intermixed with
several sections of moderate to difficult boulder scrambling. In addition,
there are a couple of 15' sections of class III (see glossary) down-climbing.

Colorful rocks brighten the lower half of the canyon. The shades of
pink, orange, red, and yellow are the natural results of mineral presence.

Route: Upon reaching Pine City, follow the road-trail to the left (NW) of
the boulder piles. The road-trail (marked on the topographical map) continues past several mine shafts and ends on a ridge. (Climb to the top of
the knoll (NW) for views down into Twentynine Palms Valley and beyond.)

From the end of the road, drop NE down over the ridge. Continue north
down a gully to intersect the canyon wash. Travel northeast down the
canyon. Upon exiting the canyon, continue to follow the wash 1.5 miles to
intersect Park Boulevard near the North Entrance Exhibit.

8. DESERT QUEEN MINE

Type: trail/road-trail, day
Mileage: 1.4 (round-trip)
Time: 1 hour
Difficulty: easy - moderate
Elevation Extremes: 4300' - 4460'   **Difference:** 160'
Starting and Ending Points: Pine City Backcountry Board (4436')
Topo Maps: Queen Mtn. 7.5'   **Appendix D Map:** # 4

Summary: The Desert Queen Mine was one of the most profitable and
longest-operating (1895-1961) mines in the park area. According to the US
Bureau of Mines, it produced 3,845 ounces of gold that, in turn, yielded
several million dollars. Machinery, stone building ruins, and several mine
shafts dot the hillsides in a concentrated area above the Desert Queen Wash.

A hiker examines old mining equipment along the Desert Queen Mine Trail.

Today steel grates block most of the shafts. Look through the grates to view the shaft structure and some of the equipment used within the mines.

The trail to the mine crosses a ravine. While in the ravine, take some time to walk up the wash and explore the picturesque canyon. The wash winds below steep rocky walls as it travels through trees and giant boulders.

Route: Follow the trail 300 yards from the east side of the parking lot to a junction. The main trail branches off and heads south (right). However, it is worth continuing straight an additional 0.1 miles to an overlook above the mine area. A sign at this overlook explains the history of the mine.

To reach the mine, head south at the trail junction. A stone building ruin, remnant of the mining days, is located beside the trail near the junction. The trail continues past the ruin and down to a ravine. Cross the wash to find the trail leading up to the mines. Most of the shafts are near the top of the ridge.

9. DESERT QUEEN WASH

Type: trail/x-country, day
Mileage: 3.5 miles (one-way)
Time: 2-3 hours
Difficulty: moderate, moderately difficult
Elevation Extremes: 3875' - 4440'   **Difference:** 565'
Starting Point: Pine City Backcountry Board (4436')
Ending Point: Park Blvd., two paved pullouts, 1 mile west of Pinto Wye (3884')
Topo Maps: Queen Mtn. 7.5'   **Appendix D Map:** # 4 & 8

Summary: The walk down Desert Queen Wash is a pleasant addition to the Desert Queen Mine hike (preceding hike). The sandy wash travels east through a ravine lined with large oak, juniper, willows, and pine trees. There is some moderate boulder scrambling in the lower half of the wash.

71

The wash passes John's Camp, the Ming Mine (circa 1931), and other pioneer mining camps as it continues downhill for three miles. At John's Camp, the route leaves the wash and follows a road-trail across relatively flat terrain to Park Boulevard.

Route: Follow the Desert Queen Mine trail south down into the sandy ravine. Travel down the ravine, which leads generally north and then east. The first significant mining camp is about 1.5 miles down the wash. To locate this site, watch for the remains of a model "T" pickup truck. It sits about 50' beyond the right bank of the wash. The cabin remains, located on the southeast side of a large boulder, are 75' farther down the wash from the truck.

To locate John's Camp, continue down the wash another 1/2 mile to the Ming Mine. (Mine shafts are dangerous; maintain a safe distance from their openings. Refer to Chapter 3, "Hazards-Use Caution.") Watch for the bluish gray tailings pile on the left bank about 50' above the wash. This marks the Ming Mine. From the mine, continue 400' down the wash then exit the wash on the right side. John's Camp is in this area between the wash and the bottom of the ridge. Look for the cement platform, scattered metal debris, rock inscriptions, and a metal and rock stove.

Locate the overgrown road-trail that parallels the bottom of the ridge. Follow the road-trail southeast then south (right) around the nose of the ridge. The road-trail disappears in a wash. Travel up the wash about 100 yards. At this point the wash bends around the ridge and heads west. The road-trail heads south up a less obvious drainage. (Look beyond the row of bushes to spot the continuing road-trail.)

The road-trail travels 100' up this secondary drainage then heads ESE up over the bank. The remainder of the road-trail is fairly easy to follow. Travel southeast down the road-trail and exit onto Park Boulevard between the two paved pullouts.

10. EAGLE CLIFF HILLS / MINE

Type: x-country, day/overnight
Mileage: 3.5 miles (round-trip)
Time: 2 - 3 hours
Difficulty: moderately strenuous
Elevation Extremes: 4300' - 4610'   **Difference:** 310'
Starting and Ending Point: Pine City Backcountry Board (4436')
Topo Maps: Queen Mtn. 7.5'   **Appendix D Map:** # 4

Summary: See Chapter 6, Hike # 7, Eagle Cliff Hills/Mine, for a complete summary. This route to Eagle Cliff Mine is longer but a little easier than the route that leaves from Split Rock. The route travels past the Desert

Queen Mine, adding another site of historical interest to the hike. Additionally, one section of the trail travels along a high gentle plateau offering an easy, pleasant way to enjoy these rugged hills.

Route: Follow the trail from the parking area to Desert Queen Mine (see Hike # 8). Travel up the road-trail to the ridgetop above the mine shafts. A continuing footpath leads east across the ridge. Look for the built-up banking of an old mining road (below a short, rocky cliff section) that leads above the eastern side of a rocky gully. Follow the trail to meet this road.

Travel north up the road-trail and continue as it contours around and beneath a boulder-covered hilltop. This 0.3-mile road section ends when it drops into a sandy wash. From the wash, look SE and locate a rock spire at the top of a rocky gully. This is the landmark mentioned in Chapter 6, Hike # 7. (If the trail becomes difficult to follow, travel up the gully to a point just below the ridgetop — about 100 yards to the left or northeast of the rock spire.) An unmaintained trail, built in 2000, leads up the left side of this gully and ends in a boulder pile. From here, a rough mining trail zigzags up the final steep section to the ridgetop.

Find the mine shaft and the pile of white mine tailings located just below the ridgetop (north side). See Chapter 6, Hike # 7 for the remainder of the route description.

Excellent views can be obtained from the Eagle Cliff Hills.

11. LUCKY LOOP

New Hike

Type: road-trail/x-country, day/overnight
Mileage: 3.2 miles (round-trip)
Time: 2-3 hours
Difficulty: moderate, moderately difficult
Elevation Extremes: 4350' - 4530'   **Difference:** 180'
Starting and Ending Point: Lucky Boy Junction (4430')
Topo Maps: Queen Mtn. 7.5'   **Appendix D Map:** # 4

Summary: This fun loop leads through a pretty canyon lined by boulder piles and large pine trees. Although it is less than a mile from the road, it has the feel of a remote wilderness. The hike begins on the Lucky Boy Vista trail then branches off into a canyon. Hiking through the canyon is relatively easy except in a few areas that require some easy to moderate boulder scrambling. Traveling under boulders and through tunnels adds adventure to this hike. The return route up another wash is equally pretty but easier. This return wash also winds through boulder piles, but there are no major wash obstructions.

An alternate return route leads down to the Desert Queen Mine trail (Hike # 8). This route leads through a section of wash clogged with large boulders. Travel involves moderate to difficult boulder scrambling.

It is well worth taking the short side trip to Lucky Boy Vista (Hike # 12). This 1/2 mile (round-trip) spur adds great views and a historical point of interest to the hike. Another quick side trip leads to a large dam (50' wide) that spans a wash. Sand has filled the area above the dam; but during wet seasons, water still flows from pipes extending below.

Route: From the parking lot, follow the trail east over relatively level ground. At 0.5 miles the trail begins a short rapid ascent up to a plateau. Halfway up the hill there is a gate that can be easily skirted. Travel about 0.3 miles across the top of the plateau. Look for a wash that leads down to the left of the trail. To take the side trip, continue on the trail to Lucky Boy Vista, then backtrack to this wash. Travel north down the wash into a little canyon.

The first boulder obstruction involves a 4-foot drop. Avoid the second obstruction, which has a higher drop, by traveling around the left side of the wash. About 150 yards farther, the wash becomes boulder cluttered. Climb through a boulder tunnel to find easier travel below. There are side drainages that intersect this wash; stay in the wash that leads down to the north.

About mile 1.7 on the loop, the wash intersects a larger sandy drainage. From here make a short side trip to the dam by traveling north down the wash about 50 yards. Backtrack to this junction and travel west up this larger wash. The return wash leads up to the parking area at the Pine City Backcountry Board.

To return via the alternate route, continue north past the dam about 1/4 mile to intersect the Desert Queen Mine trail (Hike # 8). Turn left on this trail and follow it up to the Pine City parking area.

From the parking area, travel left (south) down the road a short way to a fork. Take the left road fork and continue 1/2 mile back to Lucky Boy Junction.

12. LUCKY BOY VISTA

Type: road-trail, day/overnight
Mileage: 2.5 miles (round-trip)
Time: 2 hours
Difficulty: easy
Elevation Extremes: 4430' - 4530'   **Difference:** 100'
Starting and Ending Point: Lucky Boy Junction (4430')
Topo Maps: Queen Mtn. 7.5'   **Appendix D Map:** # 4

Summary: The hike to Lucky Boy Vista is an excellent choice for an easy overnight trip as well as for a good day trip. The trail leads to a high, level plateau that provides both superb views and some fine places to camp. The trail travels through the eastern edge of Queen Valley. It winds around through large boulders then climbs a short distance through some hills to reach the plateau. From the plateau, there are good views of the rocky Eagle Cliff Hills and views down into the rugged drainages that lead north to Desert Queen Mine.

The road-trail ends at an overlook above the Split Rock boulder maze. The Elton Mine, which consists of several vertical shafts (the majority are fenced), is also at the end of the road-trail. (Mine shafts are dangerous; maintain a safe distance from their openings. Refer to Chapter 3, "Hazards-Use Caution.")

At one time, a road-trail connected the Elton Mine with the Split Rock Road. Now the trail is mostly overgrown. However, with a discerning eye and good map and compass skills, it is possible to locate and follow the majority of this connecting route.

Route: From the parking lot, follow the trail east over relatively level ground. About halfway to the mine, the trail begins a short but rapid ascent. Skirt around an old gate and continue to the top of the hill. Follow the trail across the plateau to reach the overlook.

For overnight trips, park at the Pine City Backcountry Board and follow the road south to the Lucky Boy Junction. Leaving from the backcountry board adds about one round trip mile to the hike. (The road-trail is marked on 15' topographical maps but not on 7.5' maps.)

Chapter 9
GEOLOGY TOUR ROAD

The Geology Tour Road is an eighteen-mile (round trip) dirt road. A pamphlet, available at the beginning of the road, interprets the geology of the area. Numbered markers at pullouts along the road correspond to numbers in the pamphlet. The road travels from Queen Valley down a long alluvial fan to a one-way loop around Pleasant Valley. A rough road branches off the southeast corner of the loop. This side road travels through Berdoo Canyon to Dillon Road, which parallels the southern boundary of the park. (Note: Portions of Berdoo Canyon are frequently impassable, even with four-wheel drive vehicles.)

The Geology Tour Road begins at Park Boulevard, five miles west of Pinto Wye and 2.4 miles east of Sheep Pass. Four-wheel drive vehicles are recommended, especially for travel on the lower section of the one-way loop. However, if the roads are dry, two-wheel drive vehicles can usually travel the entire road without difficulty. Inquire about road conditions at a visitor center before attempting the drive.

Hikes starting from the Geology Tour Road travel through broad valleys forested with Joshua trees, down long sandy washes that wind through steep canyons, or up to high vistas and mountain tops. Unique geologic formations and sites of historical interest are additional hike highlights. There are backcountry boards 1.4 miles and 6.8 miles from Park Boulevard. The latter board is in Pleasant Valley. The closest campground is Jumbo Rocks, 1.6 miles east on Park Boulevard.

1. CALIFORNIA RIDING AND HIKING TRAIL
(See Chapter 11)

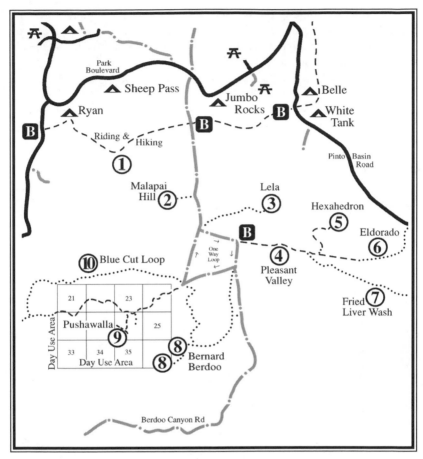

GEOLOGY TOUR ROAD

2. MALAPAI HILL (4280')

Type: x-country, day
Mileage: 1.5 miles (round-trip)
Time: 1 - 2 hours
Difficulty: moderately strenuous, moderately difficult
Elevation Extremes: 3760' - 4280'   **Difference:** 520'
Starting and Ending Point: Stop #7 (3760')
Topo Maps: Malapai Hill 7.5'   **Appendix D Map:** # 9

Summary: This is a good hike for geology enthusiasts. Malapai Hill is a volcanic dome that sits alone in the lower half of Queen Valley. A large area of columnar jointing can be viewed from either the summit saddle or from the northwest side of the hill. The summit provides good views of surrounding Pleasant Valley. A slight variation of the approach route leads to a large balanced boulder.

Route: Travel WSW on relatively level ground to the base of the hill. (Look for the balanced boulder SW from the parking area.) Ascend directly up either side of the liver-colored scree slope to attain the saddle. (Climbing the scree is easier than it looks from a distance. The scree is composed of large, relatively stable rocks.) The summit is the point located north of the saddle. To view the columnar jointing, look down on the columnar cliff from the NW section of the saddle plateau. Use caution as rocks may be loose near the plateau edge.

The approach route to Malapai Hill passes a large monzogranite boulder.

3. LELA PEAK (4747')

Type: x-country, day/overnight
Mileage: 5 miles (round-trip)
Time: 3 - 4 hours
Difficulty: strenuous
Elevation Extremes: 3520' - 4747'   **Difference:** 1227'
Starting and Ending Point: Squaw Tank (3520')
Topo Maps: Malapai Hill 7.5'   **Appendix D Map:** # 10

Summary: Lela Peak is the highest peak in the northern Hexie Mountains. A straightforward climb leads to unobstructed views of the park — across Pinto Basin to the Coxcombs, across the Hexies to Monument and Eagle mountains, and across Pleasant and Queen valleys to the Wonderland of Rocks.

Route: Wind through the boulder formations just north of the parking area. Travel northeast along the north base of the mountains. Head ENE up the second deep gully (approximately 1.25 miles from the parking area) to a plateau. Travel NE over a low ridge to reach another broad plateau. Lela is the high point on the opposite side of this second plateau.

4. PLEASANT VALLEY ROAD-TRAIL

Type: road-trail, day/overnight
Mileage: 5 miles (round-trip)
Time: 2 - 3 hours
Difficulty: easy
Elevation Extremes: relatively level
Starting and Ending Point: Pleasant Valley Backcountry Board (3250')
Topo Maps: Malapai Hill 7.5'   **Appendix D Map:** # 10

Summary: This pleasant hike travels through a flat, dry lake bed. During wet seasons, the area resembles a manicured lawn dotted with several species of desert shrubs. It is a great place for overnight camping and early-morning bird watching.

Route: The road-trail leaves from the backcountry board and heads east across the valley. There are good camping spots located throughout the valley at the base of the Hexies.

79

5. HEXAHEDRON MINE

Type: road-trail, day/overnight
Mileage: 8 miles (round-trip)
Time: 5 - 6 hours
Difficulty: moderately strenuous
Elevation Extremes: 3200'- 4000'   **Difference:** 800'
Starting and Ending Point: Pleasant Valley Backcountry Board (3250')
Topo Maps: Malapai Hill 7.5'   **Appendix D Map:** # 3 & 10

Summary: There is a variety of panoramic views from the road-trail that winds up through the mountains to the Hexahedron Mine. Although the Hexahedron Mine is not significant, a nearby rock house perched on the edge of a mountain makes this an interesting destination. Backpackers will find level camping areas with good views near the roofless rock house. (Mine shafts are dangerous; maintain a safe distance from the openings. Refer to Chapter 3, "Hazards - Use Caution.")

Route: Follow the Pleasant Valley Road-Trail (see preceding hike) to a small hill. Just before the hill, the road-trail enters a wash. Cross the wash to find the continuing road-trail. Pass through a fence at the base of the hill and continue up the road-trail to a fork. From here head N to attain the obvious mining road that ascends the mountain side. This mining road is fairly easy to follow the remaining way to the mine and rock house. (Note: The trail to the mine and the house are pictured but not labeled by name on topographical maps.)

6. ELDORADO MINE

Type: road-trail/x-country, day/overnight
Mileage: 7.5 miles (one-way) Pinto Basin Road   (11 miles round-trip to mine)
Time: 4 - 5 hours, (6 - 7 hours)
Difficulty: moderate
Elevation Extremes: 2360' (2600') - 3250   **Difference:** 880' (650')
Starting Point: Pleasant Valley Backcountry Board (3250')
Ending Point: Pinto Basin Road, wide dirt pullout on the southwest side of road; 1.25 miles northwest of Cholla Cactus Garden; 8.5 miles south of Pinto Wye (2560') or Pleasant Valley Backcountry Board
Topo Maps: Malapai Hill 7.5', Fried Liver Wash 7.5' **Appendix D Map:** # 3&10

Summary: This is not the shortest route to Eldorado Mine, but it is the most interesting. The route travels along Pleasant Valley then through the Hexie foothills to a picturesque pass that overlooks the Pinto Basin. It continues down Eldorado Wash to the mining ruins. The vegetation changes as the route descends from the Mojave Desert into the Colorado Desert. See

Chapter 14, Hike # 4b for a description of Eldorado Mine. (Mine shafts are dangerous; maintain a safe distance from the openings. Refer to Chapter 3, "Hazards - Use Caution.")

Route: Follow the Pleasant Valley Road-Trail (page 79) to a small hill. (The road-trail enters a wash a short distance before the hill. Cross the wash to find the continuing road-trail.) Continue following the road-trail past a fence to a fork. Take the right fork. Follow the road-trail through the foot-hills, up to the pass, and part-way down the other side of the pass to a wash. When the road-trail becomes difficult to recognize, enter the wash. Follow the wash the remaining distance to the mine and mining camp ruins. (To continue to Pinto Basin Road, see Chapter 14, Hike # 4b, Eldorado Mine.)

A hiker enjoys the Pinto Basin view from the pass above Eldorado Mine.

7. FRIED LIVER WASH

Type: road-trail/x-country, day/overnight
Mileage: 14 miles (one-way)
Time: 7 - 9 hours
Difficulty: easy
Elevation Extremes: 1780' - 3250'   **Difference:** 1470'
Starting Point: Pleasant Valley Backcountry Board (3250')
Ending Point: Fried Liver Wash - Pinto Basin Road (1780')
Topo Maps: Malapai Hill 7.5', Fried Liver Wash 7.5' **Appendix D Map:** # 3&10

Summary: This route leads from Pleasant Valley to Pinto Basin through a wide, sandy wash that winds below high desert mountains. Vegetation along this route gradually changes as the hike travels from the Mojave Desert into the Colorado Desert. The wash provides a colorful spring wildflower display in the height of the flower season.

Route: Travel the Pleasant Valley Road-Trail (page 79) 2.5 miles to a sandy wash near the base of a small hill. Follow the wash (Fried Liver Wash) around the south side of the hill. Continue down the wash through a mountain canyon and down into Pinto Basin. When the wash exits the canyon into the open basin, it divides into several washes. Stay along the left wall of the canyon. Travel through the basin by taking the left of all major forks in the wash. This eventually leads to a large sandy wash that crosses Pinto Basin Road.

For vehicle shuttle purposes, the exit point onto Pinto Basin Road is just west of the west-facing "Fried Liver Wash" sign (near mile 13). (Note: Flash flooding may periodically change the course of the wash. However, the wash will still cross Pinto Basin Road at some point near mile 13.)

8. BERNARD (5430') & LITTLE BERDOO (5440')

Type: x-country, day/overnight (note day use area on map)
Mileage: Mileage is to Little Berdoo. Subtract 1.5 miles round-trip for Bernard
      Route #1- 8.5 miles (round-trip)
      Route #2- 6.5 miles (round-trip) via Nard Wash, Berdoo Canyon Road
          11.5 miles (round-trip)via the backcountry board, Nard Wash
Time: 5 - 7 hours
Difficulty: strenuous, moderately difficult
Elevation Extremes: 3250' - 5440'   **Difference:** 2190'
Starting and Ending Point: Stop #14 (3520'), Berdoo Canyon Road (3760'), or
      Pleasant Valley Backcountry Board (3250')
Topo Maps: Malapai Hill 7.5', Rockhouse Canyon 7.5' **Appendix D Map:** # 10

Summary: Bernard Peak and Little Berdoo Peak are two adjacent mountains providing spectacular but different views. From Bernard there are views of the north valleys, Mt. San Jacinto and Mt. San Gorgonio. Little Berdoo provides sweeping views of the entire Coachella Valley. The hike to Bernard's summit is invigorating and picturesque. Attain Little Berdoo's summit by hiking an additional 3/4 mile (fairly easy) from Bernard's summit. A sheltered plateau between the two peaks provides pleasant flat areas for camping. There are climbing registers on both summits.

Route #1, North Wash: This is the easier of the two routes since it travels up the more gradual incline of the north wash. From Stop #14, backtrack 100 yards down the road (northeast) then walk easterly around the base of the mountains. Enter the first major wash and canyon. Follow the wash and take a left at the first fork in the wash. (In this next section of the wash, there will be a couple of low cliffs requiring class III-IV climbing.)

One-half mile beyond the fork, the canyon opens up and the wash forks again. Take the left fork and head back into a narrow canyon. About 1/4 mile from this fork, the canyon again opens up and the wash widens. Continue in the wash past this point to reach a perpendicular wash junction on the right side. (There is another wash junction on the right side before this one, but it doesn't intersect the main wash at a 90° angle.)

Leave the main wash and head SW up this side wash/gully. Follow this wash to a pass located a short distance below Bernard's summit. (Stay to the left in the narrow forks just below the pass.) From the pass, head SW up the ridge to the summit. The summit consists of two rock points with a long saddle between the points. The climbing register and benchmark are on the southern point.

Route #2, Nard Wash: Although the route up Nard Wash is shorter, it is much steeper and more rugged than the route up the North Wash. Nard is an isolated peak located between the east base of Bernard Peak and the Berdoo Canyon Road. Nard Wash descends from Bernard, travels along the west base of Nard Peak, then heads north to the center of Pleasant Valley.

The most direct access to Nard Wash is from a pullout on the Berdoo Canyon Road, 1.8 miles south of the junction with Geology Tour Road. If the roads are dry, two-wheel drive vehicles can usually travel as far as this pullout. (For overnight trips, park at the backcountry board and hike to the pullout either by way of the road or in the parallel wash.)

From the pullout, head SW about 250 yards to Nard Wash. Follow the wash south to the west side of Nard Peak, then head SW up the steep gully toward Bernard. Bernard, appearing as two peaks with a long saddle between, is the most distant peak above the gully. (There are two smaller rocky points in the center of the saddle.) Farther up the gully, Bernard disappears and a new landmark becomes prominent. A point capped by a distinctive rocky knob rises above the gully. Follow the rocky wash up to the right of this point. Continuing to take the right of all above forks in the wash leads to the pass described in Route #1.

Little Berdoo Peak Route: From Bernard's summit, Little Berdoo can be seen to the southwest. It rises slightly higher than Bernard. Drop down the southwest slope of Bernard Peak and travel southwest up and over some small ridges. Cross a small plateau (good camping spot) and climb the slope to Little Berdoo Peak. A tall stake with two square pieces of metal attached to it marks the summit.

9. PUSHAWALLA PLATEAU

Type: road-trail/x-country, day (note day use area on map)
Mileage: 6.5 miles (round-trip)
Time: 4 - 5 hours
Difficulty: moderately strenuous
Elevation Extremes: 3660' - 5200'   **Difference:** 1540'
Starting and Ending Point: Pinyon Well Parking Area (3660')
Topo Maps: Malapai Hill 7.5'   **Appendix D Map:** # 10

Summary: This hike offers a variety of vegetation, historical sites, and great views in a quiet, seldom-visited part of the park. Pinyon Well was the location of a major source of water during the mining days. A small community thrived near the well. The watering trough, water-holding tanks, wells, and building foundations that were a part of this community can be seen on the way to Pushawalla Plateau. Water still seeps from one well attracting birds and wildlife.

Just before the plateau, the road-trail passes the mine shafts and building ruins of the Pinyon Mine (also known as the Tingman-Holland Mine). This mine was among one of the first mines constructed in the park area. The mine's shafts were lined with logs rather than milled planks and beams. (Mine shafts are dangerous; maintain a safe distance from their openings. Refer to Chapter 3, "Hazards - Use Caution.")

The road-trail continues past the Pinyon Mine to Pushawalla Plateau, the highlight of this hike. The spectacular view from Pushawalla Plateau includes the Coachella Valley, from the Salton Sea to Palm Springs, as well as the park valleys and mountains to the north.

A short side trip on this hike leads to another significant mining site, the Hensen Well mill site. The remains of four stone buildings and a chimney line the sides of the wash above the site of the mill. However, it is the Chilean mill and not the building structures that makes this site historically interesting. In the early 1900's, prospectors brought ore from nearby mines

*Pushawalla Plateau provides sweeping views of the
Coachella Valley and Mt. San Jacinto.*

to this Chilean mill for custom grinding. Most milling arrastras of this era used drag stones to grind ore. The Chilean mill used large cement-filled cast iron wheels that rolled over and crushed the ore within the arrastra. Two of these massive crushing wheels are still on site.

Route: Follow the road-trail southwest from the parking area, through a canyon, to the site of Pinyon Well. Continue up the canyon to a fork (about 1.5 miles from the parking area). The right fork leads to a dead end. Take the left fork. About 1/3 mile beyond the fork, the wash/canyon turns south (left). ** Keep to the right and stay on the road-trail, which is somewhat obscure. Continue following the road trail uphill for another 0.3 miles. At this point, a rocky and steeper road-trail branches to the left and travels south.

Follow this southern road-trail uphill through the mountains. Sections of this road-trail are rough and steep but easy to follow. The road-trail fades out upon a broad scenic plateau dotted with small rocky peaks and vegetated with oaks, pinyon pines, Joshua trees, and yuccas. (Note: Following the main road-trail 100 yards past the southbound junction leads to a pass and wire-cable fence. Continuing past the fence leads down

85

through Pushawalla Canyon to the boundary and eventually out to Dillon Road in Desert Hot Springs.)

** Hensen Well: This side trip begins at the point where the road-trail leaves the wash. From this junction, continue about 125 yards south in the wash. Exit right out of the main wash and follow a smaller sandy side wash. Follow this side wash up into a rocky gully. Climb a short distance up through the rocky gully to reach the ruins and mill site. To continue on the Pushawalla route, backtrack the 0.3 miles to the road-trail/wash junction. (Note: The ruins are marked on the 7.5' topographical map.)

10. BLUE CUT LOOP

Type: road-trail/x-country, day/overnight (note day use area on map)
Mileage: 14.5 mile loop
Time: 8-10 hours
Difficulty: moderately strenuous
Elevation Extremes: 2750' - 4620'   **Difference:** 1870'
Starting and Ending Point: Pinyon Well Parking Area (3660')
Topo Maps: Malapai Hill 7.5', Keys View 7.5'   **Appendix D Map:** # 10

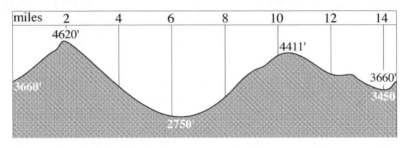

Summary: During the early mining days, the Blue Cut Wash was the original route of travel for mule team wagons. These teams travelled from the railroad depots in the low desert, over Blue Cut Pass, then on to mines located around Pleasant Valley and Lost Horse Mountain. In later years, another route, up and over Pushawalla Pass, was created to reach Pleasant Valley. Both routes have long since been closed to vehicle traffic; they are well on their way to being reclaimed by nature. The Pushawalla Pass route is readily visible in many places; however, the Blue Cut Pass route has all but vanished. A discerning eye will be able to find the slight trace of a wagon trail at the top of Blue Cut Pass.

This hike takes in both of these early wagon trail routes. The hike provides a variety of views, terrain, and vegetation. As the route ascends through a canyon to Pushawalla Pass, it travels past the historical Pinyon Well site. (See Pushawalla Plateau, Hike # 9, for a description of Pinyon

Well.) At the pass, take in the excellent views of Mt. San Jacinto before heading down Pushawalla Canyon into the low desert.

At the lowest portion of the hike, near the bottom of Blue Cut Wash, spring wildflowers are sometimes abundant. Note the change in vegetation along the way as the route leads from the low Colorado Desert up Blue Cut Wash to the Mojave Desert. A thriving group of large Joshua trees, the most notable plant of the Mojave Desert, grows on the broad flat area of Blue Cut Pass.

This trip should be planned either as an overnight trip or a very long day trip. The 1870' difference in elevation extremes, the continual up and down travel, and soft sand contribute to slow travel.

Route: The recommended direction of travel is clockwise. This puts the higher of the two pass climbs at the beginning of the trip. Additionally, it allows for easy downhill travel over the softer, sandier portion of the trip.

Follow the road-trail southwest from the parking area, through a canyon, to the site of Pinyon Well. Continue up the canyon to a fork (about 1.5 miles from the parking area). The right fork leads to a dead end. Take the left fork. About 1/3 mile beyond the fork, the wash/canyon turns south (left). Keep to the right and stay on the road-trail, which is somewhat obscure. Continue following the road-trail uphill to Pushawalla Pass. (There's a wire/cable fence at the pass.)

From Pushawalla Pass, travel 3.5 miles down the road-trail and wash to an area where the canyon opens up. At this point, there is a broad open basin on the right side of the wash and a large side wash and valley located on the left. Mt. San Jacinto looms above the main wash. Continue 1.25 miles through the open area and back down into a canyon to reach the junction of Blue Cut Wash.

The Blue Cut Wash is a major wash; however, its size is not readily obvious at the junction. (It would be easy to miss this turn.) The mouth of Blue Cut Wash is about 30-40' in width. There is a 20' high cliff on either side of the wash entrance.

Travel up Blue Cut Wash through a short canyon. There are several small side washes; stay in the main wash. The main wash forks a couple of times within the first 1/2 mile; take the right forks. The canyon eventually opens into a basin. Continue following the wash through the basin and up into Blue Cut Canyon. Within the canyon, there is a major wash/side valley that descends from the left. Do not turn left into this large side canyon; continue straight into the narrow canyon. Continue 1.5 miles to Blue Cut Pass.

Near the top of the pass, the wash forks; take the right or straighter fork. Cross the pass and follow a wash down into Pleasant Valley. Travel southeast around the base of the mountains and back to the Geology Tour Road and parking area.

Chapter 10
KEYS VIEW ROAD

Keys View Road begins from Park Boulevard, 14.8 miles from the North Entrance and 10.5 miles from the West Entrance. The five-mile road travels through the high Mojave Desert from Cap Rock to Keys View. This road is a starting point for many excellent hikes to high peaks, good viewpoints, historical landmarks, and prime wildlife habitat areas. The Juniper Flats Backcountry Board is on the west side of the Keys View Road about one mile from Cap Rock. Nearby campgrounds include Hidden Valley, 1.7 miles west on Park Boulevard, and Ryan, 0.5 miles east on Park Boulevard. See map on page 90.

1. CAP ROCK NATURE TRAIL - (See Chapter 5, Hike # 7.)

2. JUNIPER FLATS

Type: trail, day/ overnight (note day use area on map)
Mileage: 9 miles (round-trip)
Time: 4 - 6 hours
Difficulty: easy
Elevation Extremes: 4342' - 4773'   **Difference:** 431'
Starting and Ending Point: Juniper Flats Backcountry Board (4342')
Topo Maps: Keys View 7.5'   **Appendix D Map:** # 9

Summary: Juniper Flats is an extensive, relatively level area thickly vegetated with large juniper trees. Quail Mountain (5813'), the highest mountain in the park, borders the area to the north. Mt. San Jacinto, a 10,804' peak located outside the park, can be seen to the southeast.

The great views and thick vegetation make Juniper Flats a scenic spot for backcountry camping. (Note the day use area boundaries on the map.) Juniper Flats is a favorite area for the mule deer that inhabit the park. Watch for signs of deer and other wildlife throughout the hike.

Joshua trees frame Mt. San Jacinto at Juniper Flats.

The first part of the trail travels through rolling hills along the boundary of a wildfire burn. In the summer of 1999, Joshua Tree National Park experienced the largest wildfires in its recorded history. Before the fires were out, almost 14,000 acres had burned. The effects of the fire appeared devastating to those who viewed the massive fire-blackened areas that year. However, less than two years later, many of the burned areas were vibrant with life. The Juniper Flats trail travels through one of these areas. The trail begins by traveling through an area of fire spotting—live Joshua trees grow side by side with burnt trees. Farther on, the trail travels through more solid burn areas.

The trail climbs a knoll 0.8 miles from the trailhead. Look back from the knoll and notice the striking difference between the burned and unburned areas. The unburned hillside is thick with smoky-green black brush. In the burnt area below, the heavy brush is gone; it's replaced by a vibrant green carpet of annual plants (depending upon rain levels and the time of year).

Note that the Joshua trees and yucca plants are making a comeback. Joshua trees are not fire resistant; with their shaggy bark, they ignite like fire sticks. Once burned, they cannot recover. However, they can reproduce by sending new shoots up from underground runners. Notice the many Joshua tree sprouts, already over a foot high, growing beneath the fire-killed trees.

Around mile 2, the trail leaves the burn area and begins to travel through large junipers. Halfway to the flats, the trail follows a ridge offering excellent views of the Wonderland.

The trail intersects a dirt road (closed to vehicles) 4.5 miles from the trailhead. This intersection marks the end of the described hike. The road continues north another 1/2 mile to the base of Quail Mountain (Hike # 3). Continuing on the trail leads to Covington Flats (see Chapter 11, Hike # 2).

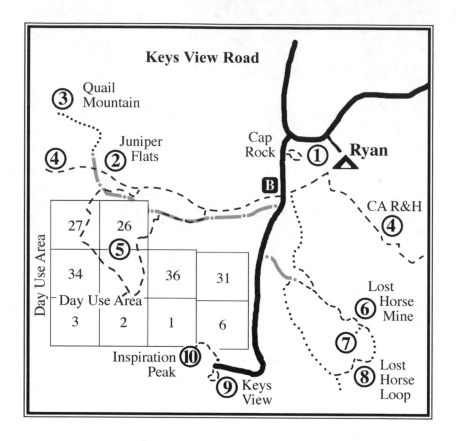

3. QUAIL MOUNTAIN (5813')

Type: trail/x-country, day/overnight
Mileage: 12 miles (round-trip)
Time: 6 - 8 hours
Difficulty: strenuous
Elevation Extremes: 4340' - 5813'   **Difference:** 1473'
Starting and Ending Point: Juniper Flats Backcountry Board (4340')
Topo Maps: Keys View 7.5', Indian Cove 7.5'   **Appendix D Map:** # 9

Summary: A relatively straightforward route leads to the top of the highest peak in the park. The ascent is either up the mountain's southeast ridge or up the southeast wash. The wash is more picturesque; it travels up through a narrow, sandy-floored canyon lined with large yuccas, nolinas, and pines.

Much of the vegetation on the upper portion of the mountain is dead and fire-scarred. A large wildland fire burned the area in 1978. On a clear day, the 360° view from the summit is outstanding. The Salton Sea, Mt. San Gorgonio, Mt. San Jacinto, Wonderland of Rocks, Lost Horse Valley and nearby small desert towns are all part of the panorama. Deer frequent the area near the top of the mountain. Look for the climbing register on the summit.

Route: Hike to Juniper Flats (see preceding hike) to the dirt road junction. Turn right and follow the road about 1/2 mile to its end. From the end of the dirt road, head NNW about 0.75 miles. Ascend either the southeast ridge or the wash just below and west of the ridge. To travel the wash route, hike up the wash to a fork. Follow the right fork up to a ridge located just east of the summit. Travel west up the ridge to the summit, which is marked by a large cairn.

Note: A social trail has developed that leads from the Juniper Flats Road-trail to the base of Quail Mountain. However, this trail does not lead to the suggested southeast ridge mentioned above. It leads to a more difficult ridge route that involves unnecessary up and down travel.

4. CALIFORNIA RIDING & HIKING TRAIL
(See Chapter 11)

5. STUBBE SPRING LOOP

Type: trail, day/overnight
Mileage: 12 mile loop
Time: 6 - 8 hours
Difficulty: moderately strenuous
Elevation Extremes: 4330' - 4960'   **Difference:** 630'
Starting and Ending Point: Juniper Flats Backcountry Board (4342')
Topo Maps: Keys View 7.5'   **Appendix D Map:** # 9

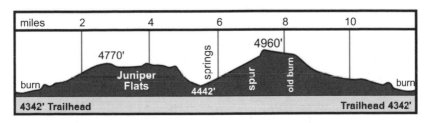

Summary: In a nutshell, this newly designated trail offers a beautiful, quiet wilderness experience in the desert. The trail travels through a variety of terrain, vegetation, and views. It leads over mountains and ridgetops and through valleys, canyons, and washes. Highlights include a rare desert water source, a dramatic vista, fire burned areas, and areas of large thick vegetation. Given the remoteness, the only man-made sounds you will hear will be from an occasional distant jet.

The first part of the hike follows the Juniper Flats trail (Hike # 2). At mile 1.6, there is a junction for Stubbe Spring Loop. Bypass this junction, and continue to a second junction at mile 3.5. Watch for a trail sign. Leave the Juniper Flats trail and head south on the Stubbe Spring trail. (This hike is easier and more pleasant when hiked counterclockwise around the loop.)

Follow the trail about 3/4 mile to intersect a dirt road. Turn right and travel 35 yards up the road to a fork. This fork is a good spot to take note of two areas with contrasting vegetation. The adjacent hills to the south have a thick covering of green pines and junipers. Now look north to Quail Mountain, which appears stark, brown and devoid of vegetation. Being the highest point in the park, Quail Mountain is susceptible to lightning strikes. Wildfires, including the 1999 fires, have burned this mountain many times over the years.

Turn left at the fork and continue to follow a road. The road soon disintegrates into an overgrown jeep trail. The trail travels along a hillside from where there are views of Mt. San Gorgonio (11,499'), Mt. San Jacinto (10,804'), and the distant Santa Rosa Mountains. A rocky descent leads to a sandy flat area. (The trail is prone to wash outs in this area so watch for trail markers or rock cairns.)

At mile 5.4, the trail enters a drainage and moves repeatedly in and out of washes for about 1/8 mile. Watch the sides of the drainages to keep track of the trail. The trail will soon climb steeply out of the wash on the left (south) side. Follow the trail up the ridge and make a sharp left turn. At this point, the trail becomes much easier to follow.

Within a short distance, Stubbe Spring comes into view on the right side of the trail. Despite the absence of surface water at the spring, there is a thick tangle of greenery. Tall grasses, sedges, and willows carpet the hillside and the drainage below the spring. Because Stubbe Spring is an important site for wildlife, the National Park Service has designated it for day use only.

The trail follows a ridge about a half-mile then descends into a wash. Turn right and travel up the wash about one mile to a signed junction at mile 7. A spur trail departs the wash on the right and leads to a must-see vista. The 1/4-mile spur ends at the edge of a dramatic precipice. Beyond the viewpoint, the ground drops steeply away revealing Fan Canyon, 2000' directly below. Look out past the canyon for views of the low desert cities and distant mountain ranges.

From the spur junction, continue in the wash a short distance. The trail leaves the left side of the wash and begins a climb to a plateau. Follow the trail across the plateau to reach an old burn area. Black juniper and pine tree skeletons still stand, but the Joshua trees are blown over and weathered gray. Compare this stark landscape to the pine-covered canyon a few hundred yards farther down the trail.

The trail winds down the canyon then heads out into the open area near Juniper Flats. At this point, Joshua trees become the prominent vegetation; the trail passes by several large trees.

At mile 9, the trail intersects a dirt road. Follow the road down to the right about one mile. While traveling the road, note that the road was a fire line for the 1999 wildfires. There are burnt trees to the left and an unmarred landscape to the right.

Look for a sign signifying the departure of the trail from the road. Follow the trail a short distance back to the Juniper Flats trail. Turn right and continue the remaining 1.6 miles back to the parking lot. (Note: It is possible to follow the dirt road back to the parking lot. However, the road is sandy, which makes walking difficult.)

6. LOST HORSE MINE

Type: trail, day
Mileage: 4 miles (round-trip)
Time: 2 - 3 hours
Difficulty: moderate
Elevation Extremes: 4600' - 5080' (5188')   **Difference:** 480' (588')
Starting and Ending Point: Lost Horse Mine Parking Area (4600')
Topo Maps: Keys View 7.5'   **Appendix D Map:** # 9

Summary: The Lost Horse Mine operation was one of the most successful gold mining operations within the park. Frank Diebold, a German prospector, initially discovered the gold strike. However, it was Johnny Lang who was responsible for making the mine productive.

As the story goes, Lang was looking for a lost horse in 1893 when he came across Diebold's mining camp. Shortly thereafter, Diebold sold his discovery rights to Johnny Lang and his father. Johnny and his new partners, Thomas and Jep Ryan (see Chapter 7, Hike # 10), started up the Lost Horse Mine operation around 1895. Over the next ten years, they processed several thousand ounces of gold.

The existing structures of this mine are among the best preserved mining structures within the National Park System. Although many of the buildings have been leveled, the significant remains of the ten-stamp mill are still standing. Several large cyanide settling tanks, stone building foundations, and miscellaneous mining equipment surround the mill. Most of the mine shafts have been fenced or sealed. (Mine shafts are dangerous; maintain a safe distance from their openings.)

The trail, once a wagon road, gradually winds up through rolling hills to the mine. Note the lack of Joshua trees and pinyon pines around the mine area. The trees were used for fuel during the mining days and have yet to regenerate.

Take the additional short, steep hike (NE) to the top of the hill (5188') behind the stamp mill. The hilltop offers good views of Pleasant Valley, Pinto Basin, Mt. San Gorgonio, Mt. San Jacinto, Lost Horse Valley, and the Wonderland of Rocks.

Alternative Route: This route leaves from the parking area, travels up through the sandy wash, then joins the Lost Horse Mine trail about one mile before the mine. The steep-sided wash lined with pines and nolinas provides pleasant hiking and a variety of vegetation. Shade offered by the pines is welcomed on a warm day.

Follow the wash ENE from the parking area. Stay in the main sandy wash rather than traveling up any of the rocky side washes. When the wash fades out, head NE 50 yards to the main trail. Travel the trail (right) the remaining distance to the mine.

Lost Horse Mine Stamp Mill

*Lost Horse Mountain offers excellent views of
Pleasant Valley and Malapai Hill.*

7. LOST HORSE MOUNTAIN (5313')

Type: trail/x-country, day
Mileage: 4.5 miles (round-trip)
Time: 3 hours
Difficulty: moderately strenuous
Elevation Extremes: 4600' - 5313'   **Difference:** 713'
Starting and Ending Point: Lost Horse Mine Parking Area (4600')
Topo Maps: Keys View 7.5'   **Appendix D Map:** # 9

Summary: Lost Horse Mountain is one of the easier mountains to climb within the park. An additional 1/4 mile hike leads from Lost Horse Mine to the summit of Lost Horse Mountain. The peak offers spectacular views of Pleasant Valley, Mt. San Gorgonio, Mt. San Jacinto, Lost Horse and Queen valleys, the Wonderland of Rocks, and part of the Pinto Basin. There is a climbing register on the summit.

Route: From Lost Horse Mine (preceding hike), follow the road-trail SE. Continue to a pass located a short distance beyond the mine area. From here head SSW (right) up the slope to the summit saddle. The summit is the farthest point to the SE.

8. LOST HORSE LOOP

Type: road-trail/x-country, day/ overnight
Mileage: 8.4 mile loop
Time: 5 - 6 hours
Difficulty: moderately strenuous
Elevation Extremes: 4600' - 5120'   **Difference:** 520'
Starting and Ending Point: Lost Horse Mine Parking Area (4600')
Topo Maps: Keys View 7.5'   **Appendix D Map:** # 9

Summary: This hike makes the trip to Lost Horse Mine longer and more adventuresome. During the mining days, this loop was a complete circle of road and trail. Nature has since reclaimed many parts of the loop, making this a partial x-country route. The route travels over a high ridge to a remote valley and the shafts and camp ruins of the Optimist Mine. (The mine shafts are dangerous, especially the vertical shaft. Maintain a safe distance from the shaft openings. Refer to Chapter 3, "Hazards-Use Caution.")

The south side of the loop provides remote, pleasant places to camp among Joshua trees and pinyon pines. A short side trip leads to the site of a Joshua tree log house — part of the Gold Standard Mine operation. All that remains of the house is a wall of logs about two feet high. (Note for backpackers: See below, "Starting from Juniper Flats Backcountry Board.")

Route: From Lost Horse Mine (see page 93), continue following the road-trail SE up and over a pass. Travel down a rough, steep road-trail to another mine (Lang Mine). Follow a foot trail that begins directly on the other side of this mine. Travel SW up to the ridgetop. (Do not follow the path that leads down to the valley floor.) Look for mine tailings (Optimist Mine), a fireplace chimney, and a road-trail on the other side of the ridge. Descend to the road-trail and follow it through rolling hills to a wash. There are pleasant camping areas at this road-trail/wash junction or southeast up the wash. The Joshua tree house is 1/4 mile (southeast) up the wash.

Complete the loop by traveling NW either in the wash or on the road-trail. (The road-trail is difficult to follow.) Both wash and road-trail exit onto the main dirt road at approximately the same location. A right turn on this road leads to the parking lot (200 yards away).

Starting from Juniper Flats Backcountry Board: Cross Keys View Road and head SE past the southern end of the nearest roadside hill. Continue SE to a wash/gully that runs north-south between the mountains. Follow the wash south. A road-trail leaves the wash on the right side and leads to the Lost Horse Mine trail. The two trails join about 1/4 mile east of the Lost Horse Mine Parking Area. It is two miles from the backcountry board to the Lost Horse Mine trail.

Keys View

9. KEYS VIEW LOOP - (See Chapter 5, Hike # 6.)

10. INSPIRATION PEAK (5558')

Type: trail, day
Mileage: 1.4 miles (round-trip)
Time: 1 - 1.5 hours
Difficulty: moderately strenuous
Elevation Extremes: 5150' - 5558'   **Difference:** 408'
Starting and Ending Point: Keys View (5150')
Topo Maps: Keys View 7.5'   **Appendix D Map:** # 9

Summary: Inspiration Peak lies a short distance from Keys View on the crest of the Little San Bernardino Mountains. Keys View is well known for its spectacular view of the Coachella Valley, Mt. San Jacinto, Mt. San Gorgonio, and the Salton Sea. The panoramic view from Inspiration Peak is even more impressive and more encompassing. The circular vista includes a more extensive view of the Coachella Valley and the Salton Sea, as well as splendid views of the park interior — the Wonderland, Queen and Lost Horse valleys, and part of the Pinto Basin.

Route: The trail starts at the NW side of the parking lot. It travels up and along a broad high point, descends to a saddle, then continues up to the actual summit. There are good views from the first high point. However, the best views are obtained from the summit of the impressive, steep-faced peak at the end of the trail. The last 50' of the trail may be difficult to follow. If you lose the trail, just scramble the remaining distance up the rock pile to the summit.

97

Chapter 11
CALIFORNIA RIDING AND HIKING TRAIL

Thirty-five miles of the California Riding and Hiking Trail traverse the park from Black Rock, in the westernmost part of the park, to the North Entrance near Twentynine Palms. As the trail travels from west to east, it passes through areas having distinct vegetation differences. It leads from the upper pinyon/juniper forests, through Joshua tree forests, to lower elevations where creosote is the predominant vegetation. The trail can be hiked either in its entirety, which takes two to three days, or in shorter sections of 4.5 to 11.3 miles. In general, it is easier to travel from west to east since the western trail sections are at higher elevations.

1. BLACK ROCK TO COVINGTON FLATS

Type: trail/x-country, day/overnight
Mileage: 7.6 miles (one-way)
Time: 3 - 5 hours
Difficulty: moderate
Elevation Extremes: 3956' - 5161'   **Difference:** 1205'
Starting Point: Black Rock Trailhead (3980')
Ending Point: Covington Flats Backcountry Board (4825')
Topo Maps: Yucca Valley South 7.5', Joshua Tree South 7.5'
Appendix D Map: # 5 & 6

Summary: The trail leads gradually uphill from Black Rock to Covington Flats. (This is one segment of the California Riding and Hiking Trail that would be easier traveled from east to west.) The first section of the trail passes through hills overlooking the town of Yucca Valley. Pinyon pines, junipers, and Joshua trees vegetate the area. The middle section of the hike, which is on a blazed route rather than a trail, travels up a sandy wash bordered by large hills. The last section of the hike parallels the Upper Covington Flats Road.
   The trail passes through some areas that burned in the 1999 summer wildfires. The stark, eerie landscape, created by the burns, is particularly

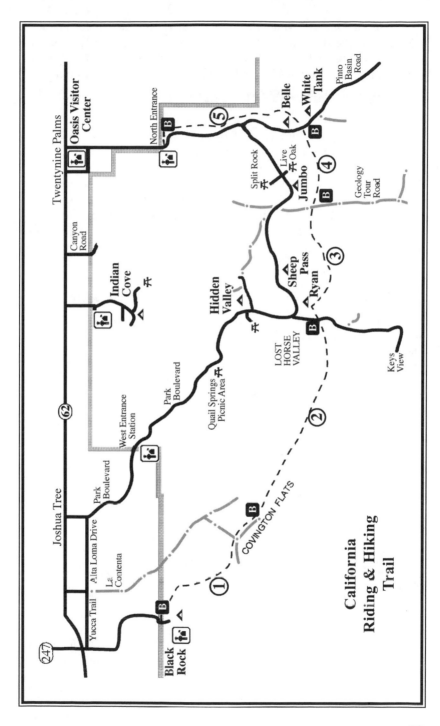

California Riding & Hiking Trail

notable in the Upper Covington section. Black skeletons of Joshua trees, oaks, and chollas dot a mostly brown landscape. There are a few splotchy areas of green annuals and only a few trees that were missed by the fire. Compare the stark burn area to the last mile of the trail. The last mile travels through large Joshua trees and other vegetation untouched by the fire.

Route: From the trailhead, hike a short distance east to a wide wash. Turn right and travel up the wash about 150 yards. At this point, the trail exits the wash to the left (east). A large sign identifies the California Riding and Hiking Trail. At mile 5.2 the trail reaches a dirt road that leads to Eureka Peak. Continue east on the trail, which parallels the road, and cross the Covington Road at mile 5.5. Continue the remaining two miles to the Covington Flats Trailhead. There are some faint trail sections particularly on the latter part of the hike. It would be wise to carry maps and a compass in case the trail markers are missing.

2. COVINGTON FLATS TO KEYS VIEW ROAD

Type: trail, day/overnight
Mileage: 11.3 miles (one-way)
Time: 5 - 7 hours
Difficulty: moderately strenuous
Elevation Extremes: 4155' - 5000'   **Difference:** 845'
Starting Point: Covington Flats Backcountry Board (4825')
Ending Point: Juniper Flats Backcountry Board (4342')
Topo Maps: Joshua Tree South 7.5', East Deception Canyon 7.5', Keys View 7.5'
Appendix D Map: # 6 & 9

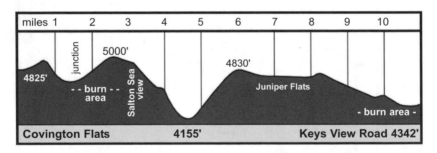

Summary: Of the five California Riding & Hiking Trail sections, this section has the greatest variety of terrain, vegetation, and scenic views. The trail leads past the remains of the largest known Joshua tree in the park, 0.1 miles from the trailhead. The tree once stood about thirty-five feet high and had a circumference of about seventeen feet at the base. Unfortunately, it shed its last live branch in 2004. The large impressive tree truck still stands amidst the pile of dead branches. The trail travels past this tree and through more large Joshua trees.

Farther on, the trail winds around a hillside through thicker vegetation—juniper, pinyon pine, and jojoba. A few switchbacks lead down the hillside to a flat valley that burned over in the 1999 summer wildfires. Distant Mt. San Gorgonio rises above this valley. The trail continues up out of the valley to a plateau then travels along a high ridge. From the ridge, the view of the Salton Sea is excellent. A rocky trail descends the ridge, travels along a lower hillside, then zigzags up to Juniper Flats. Tracks and droppings indicate the elusive bighorn sheep frequent this area. (Note: A few short trail sections may be difficult to follow. Look for cairns or rock piles that mark the route through the washes and burn areas and over rocky terrain.)

Juniper Flats (see Chapter 10, Hike # 2) is another highlight of this hike. Large juniper trees abound in this scenic, relatively level area. At Juniper Flats, the trail crosses a dirt road (closed to vehicles) then continues gradually downhill the remaining 4.5 miles to Keys View Road. This last portion of the trail follows along a ridge that offers excellent views of the Wonderland.

3. KEYS VIEW ROAD TO GEOLOGY TOUR ROAD

Type: trail, day/overnight
Mileage: 6.6 miles (one-way)
Time: 3 - 4 hours
Difficulty: moderate
Elevation Extremes: 4340' - 4550'   **Difference:** 210'
Starting Point: Juniper Flats Backcountry Board (4342')
Ending Point: Geology Tour Road Backcountry Board (4493')
Topo Maps: Keys View 7.5', Malapai Hill 7.5'   **Appendix D Map:** # 9

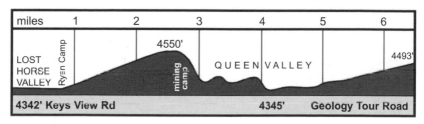

Summary: This trail travels over a low pass between Ryan and Lost Horse mountains. The trail leads gradually up from Lost Horse Valley to the pass then gradually down the other side of the pass into Queen Valley. East of the pass, the trail travels by a horizontal mine shaft (unsafe for entry) located

101

thirty feet to the right of the trail. Look for the remains of a prospector camp located a short distance beyond the mine and on the opposite side of the trail.

This is just one of the many mining camp ruins found throughout the park. A few lucky and industrious desert pioneers did discover rich deposits of gold as is evidenced by the success of the Lost Horse and Desert Queen mines. However, most pioneer prospectors were hardly able to scrape out a meager existence. Ruins, such as this one, are all that remain of their unfulfilled dreams of gold and great wealth.

From the ruins, the trail continues across Queen Valley to the Geology Tour Road. (The trail can also be accessed from Ryan Campground. Starting from the campground shortens the hike by 3/4 of a mile.) For overnight trips, park all vehicles at the backcountry board rather than at Ryan Campground.

4. GEOLOGY TOUR ROAD TO PINTO BASIN ROAD

Type: trail, day/ overnight
Mileage: 4.5 miles (one-way)
Time: 2 - 3 hours
Difficulty: easy
Elevation Extremes: 3900'- 4493'   **Difference:** 593'
Starting Point: Geology Tour Road Backcountry Board (4493')
Ending Point: Twin Tanks Backcountry Board (3900')
Topo Maps: Malapai Hill 7.5'   **Appendix D Map:** # 8

Summary: This is the shortest and easiest section of the California Riding & Hiking Trail. It travels gradually downhill as it leads from west to east across Queen Valley. About 1.7 miles from Geology Tour Road, the trail passes near large rock formations. The rocks provide a scenic and sheltered place to camp or have lunch. The remainder of the trail travels through the open valley where there are good views of two outstanding and unique areas in the park—Pinto Basin and the distant Coxcomb Mountains. (See Chapters 14 and 17.)

Pinto Basin is an immense basin measuring close to 200 square miles. It is mostly untouched by road or human foot. Although two roads do travel through parts of the area, most of the basin remains a wilderness. Beyond Pinto Basin is the Coxcomb Mountain Range, a wilderness of remote, highly distinctive, rugged peaks.

5. PINTO BASIN ROAD TO NORTH ENTRANCE

Type: trail/x-country, day/overnight
Mileage: 7.3 miles (one-way)
Time: 3 - 4 hours
Difficulty: easy
Elevation Extremes: 2840' - 3900'   **Difference:** 1060'
Starting Point: Twin Tanks Backcountry Board (3900')
Ending Point: North Entrance Backcountry Board (2880')
Topo Maps: Malapai Hill 7.5', Queen Mtn. 7.5'   **Appendix D Map:** # 8

Summary: The final section of the California Riding & Hiking Trail is almost all downhill. The trail parallels the road its entire length, although it is far enough removed to obscure the sound of motors. The most interesting part of the trail is the first three miles. This section travels along the base of Belle Mountain and through rock piles located east of Belle Campground.

Look for an interesting rock formation, appropriately named Bull's Eye Rock, at mile 1.8. From the correct angle, Bull's Eye Rock looks like a giant calf's head. The eye is a perfectly round hole through the rock. By itself, the eye appears like a giant shotgun slug hole. Locate the formation by finding a rock pile that sits a few feet off the trail's east side. The Bull's Eye is just behind and northeast of this rock pile.

From mile 3 to the end, the trail travels through or adjacent to a wash. The trail is prone to washouts; carry a topographical map and compass in case you lose the trail.

A hiker's head creates a pupil in the Bull's Eye.

Chapter 12
INDIAN COVE
FORTYNINE PALMS

The Indian Cove / Fortynine Palms area is located along the northern edge of the park. Since the area is generally warmer and more sheltered than other parts of the park, it is popular during the winter. Two roads lead to this area off Highway 62 — Indian Cove Road and Canyon Road. Indian Cove Road leads to a ranger station, picnic area, and a 110 site reservable campground. Hikes leaving from Indian Cove lead into the Wonderland of Rocks or skirt around the Wonderland through gentler terrain. The Indian Cove Back-country Board is on the west side of the road, 1/2 mile south of the ranger station. Canyon Road is 1.7 miles east of Indian Cove Road. The trail at the road's end leads to a beautiful oasis and a wild, rocky canyon.

1. BOY SCOUT TRAIL - (See Chapter 7, Hike # 7.)

2. INDIAN COVE NATURE TRAIL
(See Chapter 5, Hike # 2.)

3. GUNSIGHT LOOP

Type: x-country, day
Mileage: 2.75 mile loop
Time: 4 hours
Difficulty: strenuous, difficult (+)
Elevation Extremes: 3300' - 4100'   **Difference:** 800'
Starting and Ending Point: Indian Cove Campground, west end (3334')
Topo Map: Indian Cove 7.5'   **Appendix D Map:** # 7

Summary: This is an adventuresome hike that covers some beautiful, but extremely rugged terrain. The route travels 800' up a steep draw filled with slick rock canyons and boulder caves. The route is not recommended for anyone less than proficient in serious boulder scrambling. Following the ascent, the route travels through a high, relatively level, rock-enclosed valley. It descends another draw that is nearly as rugged as the first.

In the upper valley, the route passes beneath a cave located about 100' above the wash in a rock formation. The cave, which is now empty, may have been used by early Native Americans who roamed through this area on hunting and food gathering expeditions. These ancient people often used rock overhangs and caves for temporary shelter and storage. (The climb into the cave is treacherous and not recommended.)

From the descent route, there are periodic views out beyond the rocky maze of the Wonderland into the gentler desert that houses local communities. In the last 3/4 miles of the hike, the terrain flattens out. The wash is wider, filled with sand, and forested with short willows.

Route: Drive to the west end of the campground and park at the end of the loop. Look SW toward the obvious low notch known as the "Gunsight". The route travels up through the boulder filled canyon, Gunsight Canyon, to the top of this notch. (The climb is every bit as difficult as it looks.)

Indian Cove / Fortynine Palms

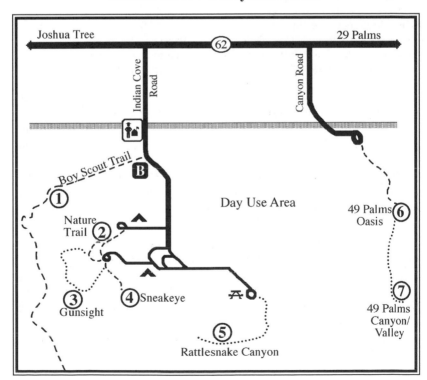

From the parking lot, follow the road-trail southwest about 100 yards. Leave the road-trail and continue southwest to the base of Gunsight Canyon. Scramble up the canyon.

About 3/4 miles from the base, the canyon opens into a small valley. Travel a short ways up the wash to a fork. Take the right fork. Continue traveling 1/2 mile up the wash, which tops out in a gentle, high valley. Travel to the right around the rock formations over relatively level ground.

A wash will soon begin a gentle descent to the north. The gentleness is short lived. Travel again becomes extreme as the wash descends nearly 600' in about 1/4 mile. At the bottom of the steep descent, follow the wash (now gentle) down through the willow trees to the intersection with the nature trail wash. Turn right at the wash junction and travel about 100' up the wash to the nature trail signs. Follow the nature trail east back to the parking lot.

4. SNEAKEYE SPRING

Type: road-trail/x-country, day
Mileage: 1 mile (round-trip)
Time: 1 hour
Difficulty: moderate, difficult
Elevation Extremes: 3334' - 3500'   **Difference:** 166'
Starting and Ending Point: Indian Cove Campground, west end (3334')
Topo Map: Indian Cove 7.5'   **Appendix D Map:** # 7

Summary: Before 1940, Sneakeye Spring was a productive water source. Today, the only water found in the area is rainwater caught in the series of granite slab potholes that surround the spring site. However, some man-made remains of a water collection system indicate the spring was not always dry.

These remains include a couple of low cement walls (tanks) with a valve protruding from one of the cement walls. In addition, there is a rock and cement tank in the wash at the base of the draw. Undoubtedly, it was used to collect the piped spring water.

According to local legend, bootleggers used this water collection system during the prohibition days. A traveling freight man, known as Iron Wheel Johnson, picked up the illegal booze and brought it down to the cities to sell.

The hike to Sneakeye Spring is short but a little challenging. It involves scrambling up through a rocky draw filled with large boulders. The spring site and the remains of the water collection system are in a small, flat, open area vegetated with scrub oak trees. Travel beyond the spring site becomes more difficult.

Route: Drive to the west end of the campground and park at the end of the loop. Follow the road-trail that leads southwest from the parking lot. It curves around a rock formation, then heads southeast. The road-trail follows along a ridgetop and leads to the end of a ridge. From here, a narrower trail leads down and south about 50' to a high point above the wash. Sneakeye is located (S) up in the rocky draw on the other side of the wash.

Continue on a footpath SSW down the ridge to the bottom of the wash. (The rock and cement still tank is located in the wash bottom. Look under an oak tree about 25' west of the rocky draw.) Cross the wash and scramble up the draw about 100 vertical feet. Follow a shallow slick-rock slot canyon. It curves around to the right and leads to the open area vegetated with oaks.

5. RATTLESNAKE CANYON

Type: x-country, day
Mileage: 3 miles (round-trip)
Time: 3 hours
Difficulty: strenuous, difficult
Elevation Extremes: 3017' - 3400'   **Difference:** 383'
Starting and Ending Point: Indian Cove Picnic Area (3017')
Topo Maps: Indian Cove 7.5'   **Appendix D Map:** # 7

Summary: The highlight of Rattlesnake Canyon is a polished slot canyon located 0.4 miles up the wash from the picnic area. After rainstorms, water swirls in large potholes as it cascades down through the multi-leveled canyon. Some of these potholes retain water throughout much of the year.

For many hikers, the slot canyon and adjacent smooth slab are a natural barrier to further travel. Those adventurous few who continue to the upper reaches of Rattlesnake Canyon will discover a lovely sandy wash set between steep, rocky walls. Cottonwoods and other leafy deciduous trees brighten this isolated upper canyon and provide seasonal shade. (Rattlesnake Canyon is prone to dangerous flash floods. Refer to Chapter 3, "Hazards - Use Caution.")

Route: Head east from the Rattlesnake Canyon signboard to a large wash. Go south up the wash, which soon becomes cluttered with boulders. (To reach the base of the slot canyon, some moderate boulder scrambling is necessary.) Continue up the wash through the boulders to reach a rocky alcove. This appears to be a dead end. Don't mistake this rocky alcove, which has several large potholes, for the slot canyon. The slot canyon lies just above the alcove.

Climb around the alcove along the right side. Scramble up the boulder slabs, choosing the gentlest slope to the far right of the alcove. Go up about 40 feet in elevation to reach a flatter area at the base of the true slot canyon. Drop left down into the wash near the base of the slot canyon to see the landmarks for the continuing hike.

Giant nolinas dwarf a hiker in a canyon above Indian Cove.

Look to the right of the slot canyon for a slab streaked with black desert varnish. Travel up along the right edge of the slab and under a large, left-pointing boulder. Hike up a rocky, bushy drainage about 50 yards to a narrow gap in the rocks. Traveling through the gap (partially hidden by oak trees) leads to the top of the slot canyon. More scrambling above the slot canyon is necessary to reach the upper sandy wash.

6. FORTYNINE PALMS OASIS

Type: trail, day
Mileage: 3 miles (round-trip)
Time: 2 - 3 hours
Difficulty: moderately strenuous
Elevation Extremes: 2720' - 3080'   **Difference:** 360'
Starting and Ending Point: end of Canyon Road (2720')
Topo Maps: Queen Mtn. 7.5'   **Appendix D Map:** # 7

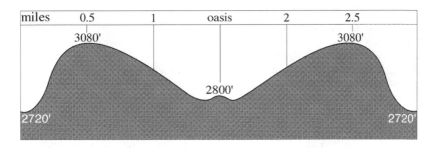

Summary: Fortynine Palms Oasis is one of five oases in the park. The well-maintained trail to this oasis ascends to a ridge above the parking lot. Look for a concentrated display of barrel cacti on top of the ridge. The thick red spines and the large, round shape of the plant itself make this cactus easy to identify. After winding around the ridgetop, the trail steeply descends the other side of the ridge to the oasis.

The oasis is in a rocky canyon. Over fifty native fan palms tower above clear pools of water lined with emerald-green algae. Under the oasis canopy, there are large polished boulders that provide a place to rest and enjoy the natural life and sounds of this miniature ecosystem.

The palm trees at Fortynine Palms Oasis look noticeably different from the trees at the other oases in the park. The trunks of many of the trees are black, and the characteristic skirts of dead palm fronds are absent. This is the result of four fires that have swept through the area since 1940. The black palm trunks supporting a bright green canopy give this oasis a unique beauty.

Note: Some thoughtless hikers have carved into some of the palm trunks. This distracts from the natural beauty of the area. Please don't contribute to the graffiti. Hopefully some of the scars will heal with time.

7. FORTYNINE PALMS CANYON / VALLEY

Type: trail/x-country, day
Mileage: 6 miles (round-trip) to beginning of valley
          10 miles (round-trip) to end of valley
Time: 6 - 9 hours
Difficulty: strenuous, difficult (+)
Elevation Extremes: 2720' - 4150'   **Difference:** 1430'
Starting and Ending Point: end of Canyon Road (2720')
Topo Maps: Queen Mtn. 7.5'   **Appendix D Map:** # 7

Summary: This route quickly gains elevation as it ascends through a rugged, narrow canyon above Fortynine Palms Oasis. Eventually the walls of the canyon open to a high, picturesque valley where the coyote and the elusive desert bighorn find an isolated retreat. This hike should only be attempted by those confident in boulder scrambling. Technical rock climbing skills and equipment are also suggested due to a couple of slick rock cliffs that bar the wash. The highest cliff, which has a rocky landing below, is 15-20' high.

Route: Hike the trail from the parking lot to Fortynine Palms Oasis (see preceding hike). From the oasis, travel south up the canyon. Look for a spring, more palms, and a collection of willows growing in the wash 1/2 mile above the oasis.

Beyond the spring, the canyon narrows and boulder scrambling becomes more difficult. The canyon exits into a small open area. Continue past the open area by traveling in the narrow canyon to the left. Emerge from the canyon into a long, wide valley. Small rocky hills dot the center of this broad valley. To reach the end of the valley, follow the wash along the northeast edge of these hills.

Chapter 13
BLACK ROCK / COVINGTON FLATS

The Black Rock / Covington Flats area lies within the most western portion of the park. It is an area of high elevation where some of the largest Joshua trees grow in dense concentrations. Two roads lead into the area. Joshua Lane in Yucca Valley leads to Black Rock Visitor Center, Ranger Station, and Campground (a 100 site reservable campground with running water and flush toilets). Black Rock is the start of the California Riding and Hiking Trail. Other hikes from Black Rock include hikes to high peaks that have excellent views and routes along sandy washes that wind through picturesque canyons.

The second access to this area is La Contenta Road. This road heads south off Highway 62 in Yucca Valley. La Contenta leads to a system of dirt roads that travel through Covington Flats. Hikes from this area lead to Black Rock, travel down a lush canyon, or lead east through isolated mountains and valleys. There are backcountry boards at the entrance to Black Rock Campground and at the east end of Upper Covington Flats. Facilities at Black Rock may be closed during some months of the year. During these closures, the area remains open to hiking. See map on page 112.

1. HIGH VIEW NATURE TRAIL - (See Chapter 5, Hike # 1.)

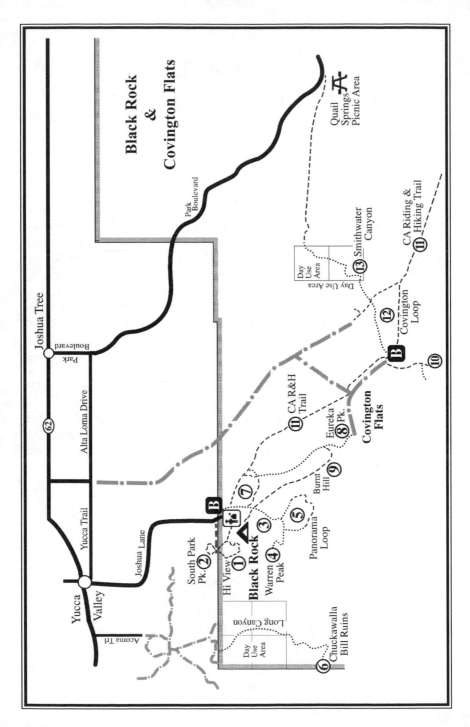

2. SOUTH PARK PEAK (4395')

Type: trail, day
Mileage: 0.7 mile loop
Time: 1 hour
Difficulty: moderate
Elevation Extremes: 4140' - 4395'   **Difference:** 255'
Starting and Ending Point: South Park Parking Area (4140')
Topo Maps: Yucca Valley South 7.5'   **Appendix D Map:** # 5

Summary: This short loop trail is actually just outside the park. However, its proximity to Black Rock Campground makes it worthy of inclusion in this book. The Yucca Valley Parks District manages and maintains this trail.

The trail leads a short distance up the peak which sits on the edge of the Morongo Basin. From the summit, there are unobstructed views of the town of Yucca Valley, views across to the San Bernardino Mountains, and views back into the park interior. A bench located at the summit provides a good spot to sit and enjoy the views or a spectacular desert sunset. There's a trail register on the summit.

There are several interpretive signs along the trail. Take a few minutes to learn about the plants of the Mojave Desert. Read about the special plant and animal relationships and early Indian uses of these plants. Sign the summit register.

3. BLACK ROCK CANYON

Type: x-country, day/overnight
Mileage: 5 miles (round-trip)
Time: 2 - 3 hours
Difficulty: easy
Elevation Extremes: 3980' - 4680'   **Difference:** 700'
Starting and Ending Point: Black Rock Trailhead (3980')
Topo Maps: Yucca Valley South 7.5'   **Appendix D Map:** # 5

Summary: Black Rock Canyon is a pretty, sandy-floored canyon rimmed with plentiful vegetation. The route to the canyon travels gradually uphill through a sandy wash. As the wash narrows and enters the canyon, the vegetation changes from a Joshua tree forest to a forest of juniper, oak, and pinyon pine. The wash forks at two points in the canyon. Most of the forks gradually lead out of the canyon to higher open areas.

Route: Follow the trail a short distance from the trailboard to Black Rock Canyon Wash. Follow the wash south. The wash branches in several places; stay in the obvious, larger wash. About 3/4 miles up the wash, the wash

113

widens, becomes bushy, and forks. Take the left fork. Continue up the wash to Black Rock Spring (usually just a damp spot in the canyon). The canyon section of the route is 1.5 miles from the trailhead.

4. WARREN PEAK (5103')

Type: x-country, day/overnight
Mileage: 6 miles (round-trip)
Time: 3 - 4 hours
Difficulty: moderately strenuous
Elevation Extremes: 3980' - 5103'   **Difference:** 1123'
Starting and Ending Point: Black Rock Trailhead (3980')
Topo Maps: Yucca Valley South 7.5' (1972)   **Appendix D Map:** # 5

Summary: There are excellent views from the summit of this relatively accessible peak. The approach route through Black Rock Canyon is easy. Only the last half-mile is strenuous. The sweeping views from the summit include the Coachella, Morongo, and Yucca valleys, Mt. San Gorgonio, and Mt. San Jacinto. Look for the climbing register on the summit.

Route: Follow the Black Rock Canyon Route (see preceding hike). The wash forks twice in the canyon (1.75 and 2.25 miles from the trailhead). Stay to the right at each of the forks. In the upper part of the canyon, conical Warren Peak will come into view. Follow the wash until it fades out. Climb to the summit by way of the eastern ridge (to the north). The ground is loose and rocky near the top but not technically difficult.

5. PANORAMA LOOP

Type: trail/ x-country, day/overnight
Mileage: 5.6 miles (round-trip)
Time: 4 hours
Difficulty: moderately strenuous
Elevation Extremes: 4080' - 5175'   **Difference:** 1095'
Starting and Ending Point: Black Rock Campground, near site #30 (4080')
Topo Maps: Yucca Valley South 7.5' (1972)   **Appendix D Map:** # 5

Summary: This is a great loop hike offering a variety of terrain and 360° views. The route travels though Joshua trees, pines, and junipers as it travels up and around a cluster of high peaks. From the high points on the loop, there are views of Mt. San Jacinto, Mt. San Gorgonio, the Salton Sea, Yucca Valley, and the park interior.

Horseback riders have been the main users of this route. As a result some parts of the route are steep and sandy. Traveling counterclockwise around the loop provides a little easier walking. However, route-finding is easier in the clockwise direction. The route is described in the clockwise direction.

Route: The hike begins on a road-trail that leads southeast through the Joshua trees at Black Rock. Just beyond the water tank, the hike leaves the road-trail and leads northwest on a foot trail. Watch for the post markers.

Follow the trail to a trail junction and take the left fork. Less than a mile from the campground, the trail drops into Black Rock Canyon Wash. Turn right and travel south up the wash. About 1/4 mile up the wash, the wash widens, becomes bushy, and forks. Take the left fork. Continue up the wash to Black Rock Spring (usually just a damp spot in the canyon).

About 1/4 mile beyond the spring, the wash forks again. This is the start of the loop. (Note: A large bush overhangs the right side of the wash and conceals the approach to the right fork. An inattentive hiker could easily overlook this fork in the wash.)

Continue up the left fork and follow the wash to its end in a gully beneath some mountains. A trail leaves the left side of the wash. The trail quickly ascends a steep, sandy slope to a ridgetop. A gentler trail leads up along the ridge to some high, 360° view points. The trail travels down the south side of the ridge and mountain side.

Less than a quarter mile from the ridgetop, the trail intersects a faint overgrown jeep trail. (**Left for Salton Sea View.) Travel right, down the jeep trail, to a wash. Follow the wash down to the beginning of the loop. The remainder of the hike retraces the route back to the campground.

** Salton Sea View: Turn left at the jeep trail intersection. Travel up the jeep trail about 150 yards to a knoll.

6. LONG CANYON /
CHUCKAWALLA BILL RUINS

Type: x-country, day/ overnight (note day use area on map)
Mileage: 10 miles (round-trip)
Time: 6 hours
Difficulty: moderate
Elevation Extremes: 2510' - 4340'   **Difference:** 1830'
Starting and Ending Point: Radio Tower Road (4340')
Topo Maps: Yucca Valley South 7.5'   **Appendix D Map:** # 5

Summary: Long Canyon winds down through high mountains. Except for the first half mile, the route gradually loses elevation and walking is easy. The first half mile is rocky and a bit steep but still not difficult.

Long Canyon continues all the way to Desert Hot Springs on the south boundary of the park. Hiking one way from the north to the south boundary is an easier alternative to this trip. This would shorten the trip by one mile and eliminate the uphill return trip. Unfortunately, it would require a long vehicle shuttle.

About half way down Long Canyon, there is a side wash that leads west to a spring and some ruins. A prospector named Bill Simmons once occupied the roofless stone cabin. Over the fireplace in the cabin, Simmons wrote his nickname and the year in the cement —"Chuckawalla Bill 1934". Simmons obtained this nickname when a visiting priest dined with him at the cabin. Simmons trapped and served a chuckwalla and tried to pass it off as fish.

Bill tapped water from a spring not far from the cabin. Today the spring is unreliable as a source of water. However, during wet seasons, water trickles down the slick rocks. Green grasses and bushes thrive in the small, narrow gorge that houses the spring.

Route: Many side washes join Long Canyon Wash. These side washes do not pose a problem while traveling south; however, they may create some confusion on the return trip. It is wise to blaze a route with rock cairns or sand arrows to prevent confusion on the return trip.

From the stone drainage ditch on Radio Tower Road, head south down the gully to the bottom of the canyon. Follow the wash down to the south. There is a short cliff section — about 15 feet of class III (see glossary) — not far down the wash. Avoid this cliff by traveling to the right down over a steep slope.

Continue in Long Wash to reach Chuckawalla Bill Wash, 4.5 miles from Radio Tower Road. Since there are no outstanding landmarks, locating Chuckawalla Bill Wash can be tricky. Keeping track of progress on a topographical map is the surest way to locate the ruins.

In addition, use the distant Santa Rosa Mountains as a landmark as follows: Pass through a slick rock chute in the wash. A short distance past the chute, the Santa Rosa Mountains become visible. Farther down the wash they disappear. Eventually, they will reappear at a point where the wash significantly widens. Continue 1/4 mile further down the wash to reach Chuckawalla Bill Wash.

Look for a slight trace of road on the right (north) of this wide side wash. There may be some pieces of wood and metal embedded in the sand at the wash junction. (Recent flash flooding may have carried the metal and wood away.) Head west up Chuckawalla Bill Wash to the ruins. The spring is about 100 yards past the ruins.

To exit the hike on the south boundary, return to the main wash and follow Long Canyon south. There is a dirt road just past the boundary fence.

Access to this road is from Desert Hot Springs. (Drive north off Dillon Road onto Wide Canyon Road. At the end of Wide Canyon Road, follow an unnamed road north to the boundary.) The 7.5' topographical map for this lower portion of the hike is Seven Palms Valley.

7. SHORT LOOP

New Hike

Type: trail/x-country, day/overnight
Mileage: 4 miles (round-trip)
Time: 2 - 3 hours
Difficulty: moderate
Elevation Extremes: 3978' - 4500'   **Difference:** 522'
Starting and Ending Point: Black Rock Trailhead (3980')
Topo Maps: Yucca Valley South 7.5', Joshua Tree South 7.5'
Appendix D Map: # 5

Summary: The Short Loop provides a variety of terrain, vegetation, and views. The trail passes through hills, washes, ravines, and valleys. It travels over ridges and a low pass between two mountains. The vegetation is particularly thick and noteworthy on the latter portion of the hike. Many large pinyon pines, oaks, and junipers are interspersed with the more typical vegetation of the Mojave Desert such as black brush, yuccas, and Joshua trees. A short section of the loop known as the Fault Trail travels near a crevice believed to be the result of the 1992 Landers earthquake (magnitude 7.6). In places, the crevice is about one foot wide and up to 18 inches deep.

Route: The first half of the trail follows the Eureka Peak trail (Hike # 8). From the trailhead, travel a short distance east to a wide wash. Turn right and hike up the wash about 150 yards. At this point, the trail exits the wash to the left (east). A large sign indicates the California Riding and Hiking Trail. Follow this trail through low rolling hills for 1.2 miles. Look for a fork in the trail marked with a post or sign for the Fault Trail, "FT." Take the right fork.

From the fork, the Fault Trail travels steeply up and down over rolling ridges. The best place to view the earthquake fault is about 0.3 miles from the fork. Stop at the last ridge saddle before heading down to Eureka Wash. Walk east of the trail about 120'. There is a crevice about 18" deep at the top of the saddle. Erosion has filled in most of the remaining fault line; however, a visible depression continues downslope from the crevice for about 30 feet.

The trail descends the ridge and passes two trail junctions for Eureka Peak. Continue following the Short Loop trail markers. The trail leads up a bushy wash, through a narrow gully, then steeply up to a pass. The descent from the pass is more gradual. While hiking down from the pass, take note

117

of and enjoy the beautiful High Desert vegetation. It is both plentiful and varied on this section of the hike. The large distant mountain that looms over the valley is Mt. San Gorgonio. It's usually snow capped through much of the year.

The trail descends to Black Rock Canyon Wash. Turn right (north) and travel down the wash and back to the trailhead.

8. EUREKA PEAK (5518')

Type: x-country/trail, day/overnight
Mileage: 5 miles (one-way)
Time: 3 - 4 hours
Difficulty: moderately strenuous (uphill)
Elevation Extremes: 3980' - 5518'   **Difference:** 1538'
Starting Point: Black Rock Trailhead (3980')
Ending Point: Eureka Peak Parking Area (5450')
Topo Maps: Yucca Valley South 7.5', Joshua Tree South 7.5'
Appendix D Map: # 5

Summary: Access to this trail is from either Black Rock or Covington Flats. This dual access allows the option of either a one-way or round-trip hike starting from either direction. The route is described from Black Rock to Covington. The excellent views from the peak are the goal and reward of this five-mile hike. Traveling in this southerly direction makes route-finding easier.

The route travels through the hills overlooking Yucca Valley, up a wash, into a narrow canyon, through a pine forest, then up to the summit. (Open areas in the pine forest provide pleasant places for overnight camping.) The view from the summit includes Mt. San Jacinto, Mt. San Gorgonio, and the Coachella Valley. The view of Mt. San Jacinto towering almost 10,000' above Coachella Valley is particularly breathtaking. Winter snows frequently cap both Mt. San Jacinto and Mt. San Gorgonio. This provides a spectacular contrast with the surrounding desert valley and mountains.

Route: The trail leads a short distance east from the trailhead to a wide wash. Turn right and travel up the wash about 150 yards. At this point, the trail exits the wash to the left (east). A large sign identifies the California Riding and Hiking Trail. Follow this trail through low rolling hills for about 1.5 miles. Pass the trail junction for Fault Trail. (There may be a post with the markings "FT.") A short distance farther, the trail enters a major wash. A sign marks the departure of the Eureka Peak trail from the California Riding and Hiking Trail.

Make a sharp right and head south up the wash through a narrow canyon. Soon after exiting the canyon, the wash passes by two trail junctions for the

Short Loop and Fault Trail. Stay in the wash following posts and signs marked with "EP" for Eureka Peak.

Close to the halfway point, the wash winds through a beautiful, deep narrow ravine. Large pinyon pines grow from the high rocky sides of the canyon. About a mile after exiting the deep canyon, the wash forks. At this point, there should be a post marking the departure of a horse trail "BF."

Take the right fork and follow the wash to its end in a shallow gully. The trail may occasionally leave the wash to skirt obstructions. From the gully, the trail leads up to the left and over a ridge. About 100 yards beyond the ridgetop, another horse trail departs and heads north (left). This junction may not be marked. Follow the trail that leads in a southerly direction. The trail continues up to a pass then rolls along a mountainside to reach a saddle between Eureka Peak Parking Area and the summit. At this saddle, head left 150 yards to the summit or right 100 yards to the parking area.

Note: Between Black Rock Campground and Eureka Peak, there is a spider web of horse trails. Some trails are signed while others may not be. To avoid confusion, carry a map and compass in case trail markers are missing.

9. BURNT HILL LOOP

Type: trail/x-country, day/overnight
Mileage: 7 miles (round-trip)
Time: 4 - 5 hours
Difficulty: moderately strenuous
Elevation Extremes: 3980' - 4890'   **Difference:** 910'
Starting and Ending Point: Black Rock Trailhead (3980')
Topo Maps: Yucca Valley South 7.5' (1972), Joshua Tree South 7.5' (1972)
Appendix D Map: # 5

Summary: This hike got its name because it travels through an old wildfire burn area. Burnt Hill is an obvious landmark within the burn area. The hike is described in the clockwise direction. However, route finding is fairly easy in either direction.

The first half of the hike uses the Eureka Peak Trail. It travels though low hills, pinyon pine and Joshua trees, a wash, and a narrow canyon. The loop trail departs the Eureka Peak trail a little over one mile before the summit of Eureka Peak.

The second half of the hike climbs a short ways to a pass. From the pass, the trail travels gradually downhill through open valleys and then the burn area.

Route: Follow the route description for the Eureka Peak Hike (previous hike) for about 3.5 miles. Once inside the narrow canyon, watch for a

119

brown post marked with "EP" and "BH". Turn right and follow the arrow for Burnt Hill (BH). Follow the trail up to the pass then gradually down to Black Rock Canyon Wash. There should be another post at the Black Rock Canyon Wash junction. Turn right (north) and follow the wash back to the trailhead.

Note: A side trip to Eureka peak will add 2.5 round-trip miles to the hike.

10. COVINGTON CREST

New Hike

Type: trail/x-country, day/overnight
Mileage: 3 miles (round-trip), 3.6 including Lone Tree Hill
Time: 2-3 hours
Difficulty: easy, (moderate- Lone Tree Hill)
Elevation Extremes: 4820' - 4940' (5050')
Difference: 120', (230')
Starting and Ending Point: Covington Flats Backcountry Board (4820')
Topo Maps: Joshua Tree South 7.5', East Deception Canyon 7.5'

Summary: This easy hike reaches some dramatic views within a relatively short distance. The hike leads across Covington Flats through large Joshua trees and junipers. It ends at a precipice above East Deception Canyon, a deep canyon that leads steeply down to the low desert. From the canyon rim, there are views of Mt. San Jacinto towering above the Coachella Valley and the low desert towns of Palm Desert, Palm Springs, and others. The Santa Rosa Mountains are in full view to the south and part of Mt. San Gorgonio can be seen to the west.

Large Joshua trees frame Mt. San Gorgonio near Covington Crest

Covington Crest Route / USGS Joshua Tree South 7.5', East Deception Canyon 7.5'

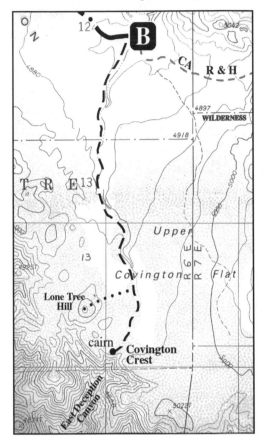

For a worthwhile side trip, make a cross-country trek up Lone Tree Hill, a little hill that lies northwest of the trail's end. The summit provides unobstructed views of Mt. San Jacinto, Mt. San Gorgonio, and the windmill valley that lies between the two mountains. Look southeast to see the Salton Sea through a notch in the nearby desert hills. The side trip adds about 0.6 miles to the trip.

Route: The unmarked trail begins on the south side of the parking lot. At 0.7 miles, the trail enters a wash; the trail continues directly on the other side. At one mile, the trail enters another wash. Travel up (right) the wash 25 yards to find the trail exiting the right side. A large cairn marks the trail's end at the precipice.

Look NNW from the cairn to locate Lone Tree Hill. It's easy to identify due to the lone, branchless Joshua tree extending above the summit. For the easiest route to the hill, backtrack down the trail 1/4 mile. Head cross-country to the summit. (Heading directly from the cairn to the hill involves extra travel up and down over ridges.) To attempt this side trip, hikers should be comfortable with navigation skills. Finding the way back to the trail can be confusing since there are few landmarks on the flats. Use a compass to avoid problems.

11. CALIFORNIA RIDING AND HIKING TRAIL
   (See Chapter 11)

12. COVINGTON LOOP

Type: x-country/trail, day/overnight
Mileage: 5.7 mile loop
Time: 3 - 4 hours
Difficulty: moderate
Elevation Extremes: 4470' - 4890'   **Difference:** 420'
Starting and Ending Points: Covington Flats Picnic Area (4670')
Topo Maps: Joshua Tree South 7.5'   **Appendix D Map:** # 6

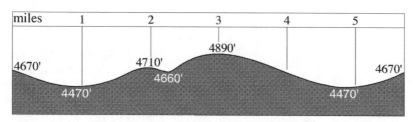

Summary: This hike makes a loop through both Upper and Lower Covington Flats. The route leads through Joshua tree and juniper forested valleys, winds up through pinyon-covered hills, and travels through a narrow canyon. The trail leads past the remains of the largest known Joshua tree in the park (located at Upper Covington Flats, 0.1 miles from the backcountry board). The tree once stood about thirty-five feet high and had a circumference of about seventeen feet at the base. Unfortunately, it shed its last live branch in 2004. The large impressive tree truck still stands amidst the pile of dead branches.

Route: Follow the trail southeast from the picnic area to a large wash. The trail is sometimes marked with posts with arrows. Look for the continuing trail on the far side of the wash. The trail intersects the California Riding and Hiking Trail two miles from the picnic area. (Watch for post #28, located near this junction.)

At the junction, take a sharp right turn and follow the Riding and Hiking Trail to Upper Covington Flats. Enter the wash located just east of the backcountry board and travel northeast (right) down through the wash and canyon. (There is no trail on this section of the hike.) Intersect the Lower Covington Flats trail and travel northwest (left) up the trail to the picnic area.

Note: Hikers familiar with earlier editions of this book, may wonder what happened to the side trip to the mine. The mine hosted the longest known section of track remaining in the park with 150' of track descending the hillside. At the base of the hill beneath the track were the remains of a drop-bottom ore cart. The 1999 wildfires took their toll; nothing significant remains at the site except two charred posts that once held the elevated track. Even the road-trail to the site is unrecognizable; thick bunches of grass, which flourished after the fire, have hidden the trail.

The largest known Joshua tree in the park grew at Covington Flats.

13. SMITH WATER CANYON

Type: x-country/road-trail, day/overnight (note day use area on map)
Mileage: 8.5 miles to Quail Springs Picnic Area (one-way)
        8.8 miles to West Entrance Wash (one-way)
Time: 5 - 7 hours
Difficulty: moderate, difficult
Elevation Extremes: 4820' - 3660' (QSPA) - 3350' (WEW)
Difference: 1160' (QSPA), 1470' (WEW)
Starting Point: Covington Flats Backcountry Board (4820')
Ending Point: Quail Springs Picnic Area (3979'), West Entrance Wash (3800')
Topo Maps: Joshua Tree South 7.5', Indian Cove 7.5'
Appendix D Map: # 6

Summary: Smith Water Canyon is a beautiful, narrow canyon. It is one of the lushest canyons in the park. The canyon walls rise steeply to high mountain peaks. In the center of the canyon, clear water cascades down through a series of smooth potholes. Several pools lined with bright green algae lie beneath small waterfalls. Tall grasses, cattails, and flowers carpet the sides of the intermittent stream. A grouping of large cottonwoods surrounds the site of a cowboy camp. At the mouth of the canyon near Quail Wash junction, there is a dense, picturesque grove of Joshua trees — a good camping spot. (Parts of this canyon burned in the 1999 wildfires; however, there is still plenty of healthy green vegetation.)

Most of the route is fairly straightforward. There are some short sections of difficult boulder scrambling in the canyon. A smooth, sloping, 20' high slab spans the wash in the lower end of the canyon. For descending this slab, a 50' length of rope is recommended for use as a retrievable hand line.

Route: From the backcountry board, follow the road-trail east 50 yards and enter a wash. Travel NNE down the wash and through a narrow canyon. Continue following the wash through the open area east of Covington Flats Picnic Area and down into Smith Water Canyon. At the mouth of the canyon (4.5 miles from the Covington Flats Backcountry Board), hike along the east side of the canyon. Find an obscure road directly at the base of a hill. Follow this road 1/2 mile to a junction where the route splits. To travel to the West Entrance Wash, head NW (left) to Quail Wash. To travel to Quail Springs Picnic Area, follow the road SE to Quail Springs Road-Trail. See Chapter 7, Hike # 3 for a description of the remaining route.

For day trips, leaving from the Covington Flats Picnic Area shortens the route by about one mile (round-trip). Follow the trail 0.9 miles east from the picnic area to the wash. (A marked trail continues across this wash.) At this point, leave the trail and travel NE down the wash into Smith Water Canyon.

Chapter 14
PINTO BASIN ROAD

Pinto Basin Road travels from Pinto Wye to the south boundary of the park and then on to Interstate 10. This chapter covers the first 22 miles of this 37-mile road. The road travels from the Mojave Desert, through a desert transition zone, then down into the Pinto Basin and the Colorado Desert.

Hikes originating from Pinto Basin Road are varied in terrain and vegetation. A hike may involve climbing to a high mountain summit, walking along an isolated sandy wash, traveling through a steep-sided canyon, playing on sand dunes, or exploring an area of historical or geologic interest. There are backcountry boards located 2.2 miles (Twin Tanks), 16.2 miles (Turkey Flats), and 21.3 miles (Porcupine Wash) south of Pinto Wye. Belle and White Tank campgrounds are 1.3 and 2.7 miles south of Pinto Wye. Cottonwood Campground is nine miles south of the Porcupine Wash Backcountry Board. (See map on page 127.)

1. ARCH ROCK NATURE TRAIL / WHITE TANK
(See Chapter 5, Hike # 9.)

1. GRAND TANK

Type: x-country, day
Mileage: 1.25 mile loop
Time: 1 hour
Difficulty: moderate, easy scrambling
Elevation Extremes: fairly level
Starting and Ending Point: White Tank Campground, near site # 9
Topo Maps: Malapai Hill 7.5'   **Appendix D Map:** # 8

Summary: Most of the cattle tanks within the park are filled with sand and maybe an occasional pool of stagnant water. Grand Tank is an exception. It is the largest of the tanks in the eastern half of the park. It usually holds water throughout the year. During wet seasons it may collect as much as 10-15' of water. A short hike leads to this secluded man-made pond.

KIP KNAPP

*Signs along the Arch Rock Trail explain the
natural creation of this large monzogranite arch.*

Route: Follow the Arch Rock Nature Trail (see Chapter 5, Hike # 9) to the "Disappearing Soil" exhibit, one stop past Arch Rock. An eroded, well-beaten path branches off the nature trail and heads ENE. Follow the path across a couple of gullies and into a boulder area. The path is easy to lose at this point. Continue across a small, bushy hollow and exit left into a larger rock-encircled area. Climb the boulders along the right side of this area and find the continuing path beyond the rocks. The path leads a short distance to the tank.

To complete the loop, follow the wash below the tank. Continue in the wash until most of the large boulder piles (along the right bank) have been passed. Climb the right bank and circle around the rock piles to the southern end of the campground.

126

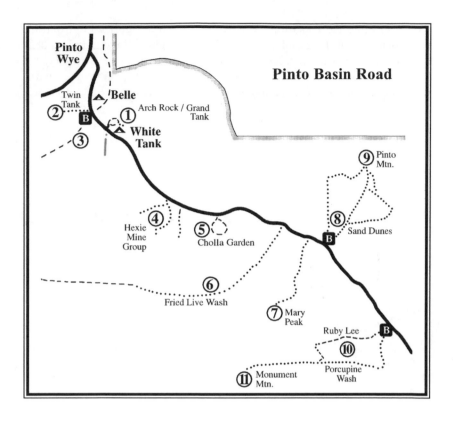

2. TWIN TANKS

Type: x-country, day/overnight
Mileage: 2 miles (round-trip) to tanks
Time: 1 - 2 hours
Difficulty: moderate
Elevation Extremes: 3900' - 4080'   **Difference:** 180'
Starting and Ending Point: Twin Tanks Backcountry Board (3900')
Topo Maps: Malapai Hill 7.5'   **Appendix D Map:** # 8

Summary: There are actually five tanks in this area. However, it is the two large man-made tanks that give the area its name. There is a series of natural pothole tanks located below the rock and cement walls of the two man-made tanks.

The Twin Tanks area consists of a maze of narrow rocky ravines, water-polished slabs, and boulder mounds. There are interesting campsite locations within or near this maze.

Route: Locate the tanks by taking a compass bearing of 245° from the backcountry board. Look for a pile of large, bright-white quartz boulders (about one mile distant) along this bearing. Hike to the quartz. The quartz boulders sit on a knoll directly above one of the tanks. From the quartz pile, locate this man-made dam (constructed of rock and mortar). To reach the second man-made tank (constructed of cement), travel about 100 yards from the quartz pile on a 300° bearing.

To explore the rocky ravines, continue in the wash past Twin Tanks or travel west from the backcountry board toward the large piles of monzo-granite boulders.

3. CALIFORNIA RIDING AND HIKING TRAIL
(See Chapter 11)

4. HEXIE MINE GROUP

Type: x-country/road-trail, day
Topo Maps: Fried Liver Wash 7.5'   **Appendix D Map:** # 3

Summary: A cluster of mining areas lies tucked within the Hexie Mountains not far from the road. The building and mill ruins and open shafts at these areas are reminders of the gold-fever days. (None of the mine shafts in this area have been secured. The shafts are unstable and very dangerous; maintain a safe distance from their openings. Refer to Chapter 3, "Hazards-Use Caution.") This section of the Hexies usually has a bountiful floral cactus display in the spring. Descriptions of the individual mine areas follow:

4a. SILVER BELL MINE

Mileage: 1 mile (round-trip)
Time: 1 hour
Difficulty: moderate
Elevation Extremes: 2560' - 2880'   **Difference:** 320'
Starting and Ending Point: wide dirt pullout on the southwest side of Pinto Basin Road; 1.25 miles northwest of Cholla Cactus Garden; 8.5 miles south of Pinto Wye (2560')

Summary: Silver Bell is the most visible of the mines in this area. From Pinto Basin Road, look for the two wooden ore bins perched on the side of the hill. The hilltop above the ore bins offers good views of Pinto Basin. Golden Bell Mine lies on the opposite side of the hill. (Travel to Golden Bell is not recommended due to the dangerous open vertical shafts.)

Route: Walk a short distance south from Pinto Basin Road and find an obscure road-trail. Follow this road-trail to a wash and then up the rocky, eroded hillside beyond the wash. (Note: This mine is pictured and labeled with "Tipples" on the topographical map.)

4b. ELDORADO MINE

Mileage: 4 miles (round-trip)
Time: 2 - 3 hours
Difficulty: moderate
Elevation Extremes: 2360' - 2640'   **Difference:** 280'
Starting and Ending Point: wide dirt pullout on the southwest side of Pinto Basin Road; 1.25 miles northwest of Cholla Cactus Garden; 8.5 miles south of Pinto Wye (2560')

Summary: This is the largest of the Hexie mining areas. Eldorado Mine is historically noteworthy because it supplied a greater variety of minerals than supplied by any other mine in the park. The remains of two concrete vats lie in the wash beneath the mine. One house structure still stands.

Route: Travel southeast from the parking area and circle around the base of the hill. Head west up the second wash and travel approximately 1/2 mile to the mine. Continuing up the wash will lead to Pleasant Valley. (See Chapter 9, Hike # 6.)

4c. GOLDEN BEE

Mileage: 3.5 miles (round-trip)
Time: 2 - 3 hours
Difficulty: moderately strenuous
Elevation Extremes: 2200' - 2840'   **Difference:** 640'
Starting and Ending Point: Two Knolls, Pinto Basin Road (2280')

Summary: This mine operated for a short period in the late 1930's. There were once many buildings at the site. Today all that remains are parts of the ore bins and a short wooden head frame.

Route: There is no parking allowed at the beginning of this road-trail. Either park at Cholla Cactus Garden and walk west 0.4 miles along Pinto Basin Road or find a safe roadside parking spot west of the Two Knolls. The beginning of the road-trail is obscure since the park has revegetated it to discourage off-road vehicle travel. To find the road-trail, leave the pavement about halfway between the two little hills. Walk toward the rock outcropping on the more western of the hills. This route will intersect an obvious road-trail within 100 yards. Travel left (south) on the road-trail. The road-trail to the mine is fairly easy to follow except in a section through the wash. The trail is easy to find on the other side of the wash.

5. CHOLLA CACTUS GARDEN
(See Chapter 5, Hike # 10.)

6. FRIED LIVER WASH - (See Chapter 9, Hike # 7.)

7. MARY PEAK (3820')

Type: x-country, day/overnight
Mileage: 6.5 miles (round-trip)
Time: 4 - 6 hours
Difficulty: strenuous, moderately difficult
Elevation Extremes: 1756' - 3820'   **Difference:** 2064'
Starting & Ending Point: Pinto Basin Road, roadside, about 15 miles south of Pinto Wye and about 15 miles north of Cottonwood Visitor Center
Topo Maps: Pinto Mountain 7.5', Porcupine Wash 7.5'

Summary: Mary Peak is a dome-shaped mountain with a 1000'+ rocky cliff face. It is the most extreme-looking mountain in the park. The mountain's rugged appearance suggests that this hike should be reserved for those with technical climbing ability. However, the climb to the summit is relatively straightforward and requires no special technical skills. The summit and ascent ridges provide commanding views of the Pinto Basin and the Pinto and Coxcomb mountains.

Route: Head S from Pinto Basin Road. Continue to the base of the narrow ridge that lies just east and parallel to a major wash. Hike up the nose of the ridge and travel along the ridgetop. The ridge, which sits directly adjacent to the cliff face, provides impressive views of the rocky cliffs.
    In a few places on the lower mountain, the ridgetop is narrow and blade-like. It is necessary to negotiate a route through large rock chunks along the ridgetop. As the ridge curves to the east, it broadens making travel a little easier. Follow the ridge as it curves around the east side of the peak then west to the summit. See the topographical map on page 131.

Alternative Routes: For a longer, gentler climb, travel up the next ridge to the east of the above described route. This route only adds about 1/2 mile to the trip one way. The drawback is the loss of the rocky cliff views on the ascent.

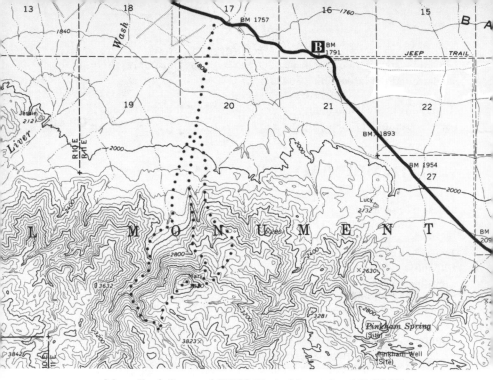

Mary Peak Routes / USGS Hexie Mountains 15' (1963)

To make a loop trip and add variety of terrain, descend southwest down the back side of the peak into a wash. Follow the wash down and around the west side of the mountain. Continue around to the front of the peak. This adds about 1.25 miles to the trip. (Note: The descent route down the wash involves traveling through a canyon over smooth granite. Use caution traveling on this slippery surface.)

8. SAND DUNES

Type: x-country, day/overnight
Mileage: 2 miles (round-trip)
Time: 1 hour
Difficulty: easy
Elevation Extremes: 1720' - 1820'   **Difference:** 100'
Starting and Ending Point: Turkey Flats Backcountry Board (1791')
Topo Maps: Pinto Mountain 7.5'

Summary: At the base of the mountains, along the northern edge of Pinto Basin, there lies a low ridge of wind-swept sand dunes, reminders of the harsh desert environment. Spring is the best time to visit the dunes. This is when dune primrose carpet the area. Look for the graceful desert lily.

131

Moved by spring breezes, the slender leaves of the lilies draw circles in the sand around the large white flowers.

Route: From the backcountry board, head NNE to the obvious sandy ridge. (See topographical map on page 133.)

9. PINTO MOUNTAIN (3983')

Type: x-country, day/overnight
Mileage: South Wash — 9 miles (round-trip)
West Wash — 12 miles (round-trip)
Southeast Wash — 13 miles (round-trip)
Time: 7 - 10 hours
Difficulty: strenuous, difficult
Elevation Extremes: 1600' - 3983'   **Difference:** 2383'
Starting and Ending Point: Turkey Flats Backcountry Board (1791')
Topo Maps: Pinto Mountain 7.5'

Summary: Pinto Mountain towers 2300' above the broad, flat Pinto Basin. The climb to the summit is rugged, strenuous, and much more difficult than it appears from the road. The summit and approach ridges provide excellent panoramic views of the Pinto Basin and surrounding mountains.

Pinto Mountain towers above the wind-swept sand dunes in Pinto Basin.

Pinto Mountain Routes / USGS Hexie Mountains 15' (1963)

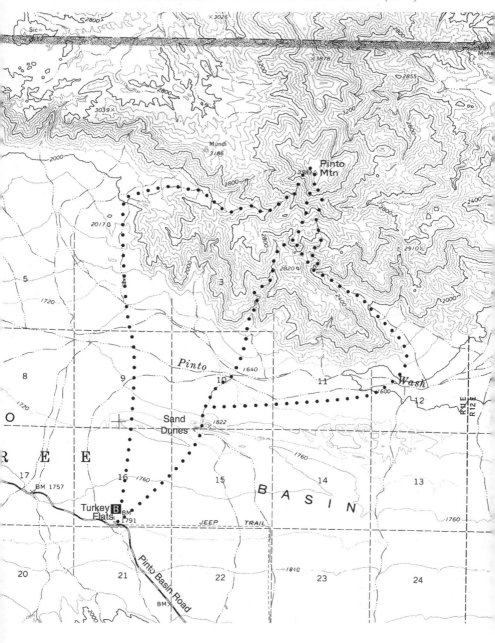

The best logic for climbing this mountain is to use the washes for approaches and gain the ridges as soon as possible to attain better views. The climb is commonly done as an overnight trip. Backpackers usually set up camp at the base of the mountain. There is a climbing register located within the 7' high cairn that marks the summit.

South Wash: This is the shortest and most rugged of the three routes. Walk NNE to the east edge of the dunes. Travel through a gap between the dunes and a low dark ridge. From here head N to the obvious canyon/wash. Look for Pinto summit above this wash.

Follow the wash as it winds up through a steep canyon. Low, smooth-surfaced rock walls span the width of the wash requiring short sections of climbing (class III). Stay in the wash for about one mile.

Watch the right ridge for an obvious change in rock color. Climb out of the wash to the right at a point where a quartz outcrop whitens the ridge. Travel along the ridgetop. Move to the right (west) of the ridge to climb up through the last rocky mound before the summit plateau. The plateau gradually rises to the summit. (See the topographical map on page 133.)

West Wash: Of the three routes described, the west wash provides the most straightforward route to the summit. Staying in the wash, rather than climbing the ridges, makes this a less-difficult trip.

Head NNW from the backcountry board to the western base of the mountain. Travel between the base of the mountain and two small hills. Head east up the wide wash. The wash eventually narrows and splits; take the right fork — the wider and less rocky of the two forks. In the upper steep section of the wash, there is another split. Keep right and follow the wash/gully the remaining way to the summit plateau. (See the topographical map on page 133.)

Southeast Wash: This route is the easiest but longest of the three routes. From the gap at the dunes (see South Wash), head ENE about two miles to a large, open wash. (The wash is not visible from the gap.) Travel up along the left (southwest) side of the wash and into a canyon. The incline is gradual with few boulder obstructions.

About 1.5 miles up the wash, the canyon narrows and bends to the northeast. Climb northwest up a steep draw to a ridgetop (the same ridgetop described in the South Wash route), or continue following the wash for a lower, longer hike. For the latter choice, follow the wash as far as possible, then continue hiking up the final steep section to the summit. (See the topographical map on page 133.)

10. PORCUPINE WASH / RUBY LEE MILL SITE

Type: road-trail/x-country, day/overnight
Mileage: 8.5 mile loop
Time: 5 - 6 hours
Difficulty: moderate
Elevation Extremes: 2400' - 3160'   **Difference:** 760'
Starting & Ending Point: Porcupine Wash Backcountry Board (2400')
Topo Maps: Porcupine Wash 7.5'   **Appendix D Map:** # 2

Summary: This is a pleasant loop hike that provides a variety of terrain and some historical and natural highlights. The route travels up an alluvial fan from where there are good views of the Pinto Basin. It returns through a narrow canyon, a good location for viewing birds and early-spring wildflowers. Historical points of interest include petroglyphs and the Ruby Lee Mill Site.

At one time, there was a small house at the Ruby Lee site. Today, the only testimony to the mill's existence is a pile of ore, a roofless rock shelter filled with debris, and an inscription, "Ruby Lee Mill Site 1935." The mill owner carved the inscription on a large round boulder that sits above the site.

A side trip from the loop continues up Porcupine Wash, through a canyon, to a broad valley. An intermittent jeep trail travels up the valley into the mountains to some mines. Monument Mountain rises above the center of the valley. The side trip from the loop to the mines is an additional 5.5 miles one-way. (Do not enter mine shafts. They are unstable and dangerous. Refer to Chapter 3, "Hazards-Use Caution.")

Route: From the backcountry board, follow the road-trail southwest about 1/4 mile to an old borrow pit. From the pit, head WSW toward the base of the hills (follow a line of green and white stakes). This route will intersect a road-trail that parallels the mountains and heads west to Ruby Lee.

The road-trail is difficult to follow in the sections that travel through the wash. If necessary, follow the wash until it separates into several smaller washes (at the end of the first grouping of hills) then locate the road-trail again. About 3 miles from the parking area, the road-trail makes a sharp bend to the right (north). From here, continue a short distance to reach the mill site located in a rocky cove.

To continue the loop, follow the road-trail west past Ruby Lee. The route beyond the mill site is not as well defined as the route leading up to the site. The center of the road-trail is largely overgrown. It will take time and a discerning eye to stay on the trail.

If it becomes too difficult to follow the road-trail, travel down any of the washes in the area. All the washes lead down into Porcupine Wash. The

135

road-trail, however, provides the easiest and gentlest route through the rugged boulder field that lies between Ruby Lee and Porcupine Wash.

The road-trail eventually takes a bend to the south, follows the base of the hills, then descends into Porcupine Wash. (Traveling west up the wash will lead to the broad valley below Monument Mountain.) To complete the loop, follow Porcupine Wash east through a canyon and back to Pinto Basin Road. The wash exits onto the road about 100 feet southwest of the back-country board. The petroglyphs are about 200 yards southwest of the road-way. Look for a large, flat-faced rock that sits on the north edge of Porcupine Wash.

11. MONUMENT MOUNTAIN (4834')

Type: x-country, day/overnight
Mileage: 20 miles (round-trip)
Time: 12 - 14 hours
Difficulty: strenuous, moderately difficult
Elevation Extremes: 2400' - 4834'   **Difference:** 2434'
Starting & Ending Point: Porcupine Wash Backcountry Board (2400')
Topo Maps: Porcupine Wash 7.5', Washington Wash 7.5'
Appendix D Map: # 2

Summary: Monument Mountain is rightly named both because of its shape and because of the summit views of the park. (The park was originally a national monument.) The mountain, which is the highest peak in the Hexie Mountains, appears as a pointed cone resting upon a broad pedestal. It is one of the most distinctive-looking peaks in the park. A long approach, followed by a steep rocky climb, leads to excellent summit views. There is a climbing register on the summit. (For an alternative route, see Chapter 15, Hike # 1.)

Route: Travel SSW 200 yards to the end of a short road-trail. Head WSW 100 yards to the deepest section of Porcupine Wash. Travel up the wash, through a canyon, to a broad upper valley. From here, Monument Mountain can be seen to the southwest. Continue following the main wash until the summit cone of Monument Mountain appears to lower beneath the closer ridges. Leave the wash and travel to the base of the mountain.

There are four distinct drainages on this side of Monument Mountain. The two center drainages form a narrow 'V'. Climb the ridge between the 'V'. This provides the most gradual and shortest ascent to the top of the first rise. From the top of this rise, drop down into a wash (approximately 80'). Walk up the wash a short distance. Climb toward the summit along the right side of the gully that descends from the mountain top. At the upper elevations, angle farther to the right (SW) for easier climbing.

Chapter 15
COTTONWOOD

Cottonwood is in the southernmost section of the park. The vegetation and terrain of the area, which is within the Colorado Desert, are quite different from that of the higher Mojave Desert. Joshua trees are replaced by smoke trees, palo verdes, and palm trees. Usually there are more flowers in the low desert than in the higher Mojave Desert. Cottonwood has some of the best spring wildflower displays in the park.

The area is most easily accessed from Interstate 10, located a few miles to the south. The area can also be reached by traveling south on Pinto Basin Road from Pinto Wye. Hikes starting from this area lead along gentle trails and washes; up rugged high peaks, as well as lower peaks; to areas of historical interest; and to the largest palm oases in the park. There is a backcountry board at the end of Cottonwood Spring Road. Cottonwood Campground, with 62 sites, is the only campground in the area. The visitor center is on Pinto Basin Road just north of the Cottonwood Spring Road. (Map on page 138)

1. MONUMENT MOUNTAIN (4834')

Type: x-country, day/overnight
Mileage: 6 miles (round-trip)
Time: 5 - 6 hours
Difficulty: strenuous, moderately difficult
Elevation Extremes: 3240' - 4834'   **Difference:** 1594'
Starting and Ending Point: Pinkham Canyon Jeep-Trail (5 miles from Pinto Basin Road)
Topo Maps: Washington Wash 7.5'   **Appendix D Map:** # 2

Summary: Monument Mountain is the highest peak in the Hexie Mountains. Excellent views of the park are the reward for completing the rugged hike to the summit. There are only a few places suitable for camping on the rocky ridges. Camping is better at the base of the mountain where the ground is level and sandy. A four-wheel drive vehicle is needed to reach the starting point of this hike.

Route: The shortest, most gradual route to the summit of Monument Mountain is up the mountain's southeast ridge. This is the ridge seen on the horizon from the starting point on Pinkham Canyon Jeep-trail. Attain the southeast ridge by heading north up one of the three lower, south-facing ridges. Climb (northwest) up the main southeast ridge to a high point. This high point deceivingly appears to be the summit. From the top of this point, look for the true summit of Monument Mountain. The true summit looks like a pointed cone.

Follow the ridge as it bends to the north and continue to the base of the summit cone. A steep, unavoidable scramble leads up the rocky cone to the summit. There's a climbing register on the peak. (See Chapter 14, Hike # 11, for an alternative route.)

2. COTTONWOOD NATURE TRAIL

(See Chapter 5, Hike # 12.)

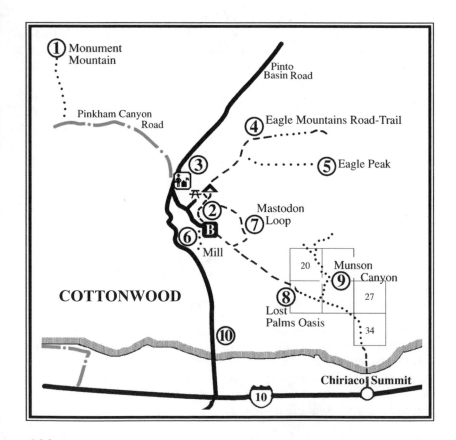

3. BOTANICAL WALK - (See Chapter 5, Hike # 11.)

4. EAGLE MOUNTAINS ROAD-TRAIL

Type: road-trail/x-country, day/overnight
Mileage: 11 miles (round-trip) to Conejo Well cutoff
Time: 5 - 6 hours
Difficulty: easy
Elevation Extremes: 3000' - 3400'   **Difference:** 400'
Starting and Ending Point: Cottonwood Spring Parking (3000')
Topo Maps: Porcupine Wash 7.5', Conejo Well 7.5', Cottonwood Spring 7.5'
Appendix D Map: # 11

Summary: This route leads over easy terrain to a remote area within the Colorado Desert. The hike is a good choice for an easy overnight trip. The road-trail travels around the base of Eagle Peak, through the western end of the Eagle Mountains, and into the south portion of Pinto Basin. The yuccas are particularly dense on the northwest side of Eagle Peak; they provide a beautiful floral display in the spring. The trail is easy to follow except in a few sections that cross or follow a wash.

Route: Hike the Cottonwood Nature Trail (see Chapter 5, Hike # 12) from Cottonwood Spring to the campground. The road-trail begins at site 17, Loop B. Travel the road-trail to a gap in the Eagle Mountains. At this point, the road-trail enters and becomes lost in a wash. Follow the wash

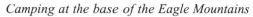

Camping at the base of the Eagle Mountains

through the mountains. Look for the continuing road-trail on the west side of the mountains. The road-trail continues along the base of Eagle Peak, passes the road-trail to Conejo Well, and then veers north. (Note: This road-trail is pictured on 15' maps, but not 7.5' maps.)

5. EAGLE PEAK (5350')

Type: road-trail/x-country, day/overnight
Mileage: 10 miles (round-trip)
Time: 8 - 10 hours
Difficulty: strenuous, difficult
Elevation Extremes: 3000' - 5350'   **Difference:** 2350'
Starting and Ending Point: Cottonwood Spring Parking (3000')
Topo Maps: Porcupine Wash 7.5', Cottonwood Spring 7.5', Hayfield 7.5',
            Conejo Well 7.5'   **Appendix D Map:** # 11

Summary: Eagle Peak is one of the most rugged mountains in the park. The climb to the summit is steep and rocky. The view from the summit is among one of the best views in the park. Pinto Basin, Mt. San Gorgonio, Mt. San Jacinto, Pinkham Canyon, and the Hexie, Pinto, Cottonwood, and Eagle Mountain ranges are a few of the highlights included in the un-obstructed 360° view.

On the climb to the summit, note the dramatic change in vegetation throughout the 2,350 feet of elevation gain. Vegetation around the base of the peak is predominantly creosote, yucca, and cholla. At the cool upper elevations of the mountain, oak, juniper, and pinyon pine abound. There is a climbing register on the summit.

Route: Follow the Eagle Mountains Road-Trail (see preceding hike) about 1.5 miles, then head E toward Eagle Peak. Navigate through the boulders and gullies to the base of the deep ravine on the mountain. (Heading toward the ravine before traveling the suggested 1.5 miles on the road-trail will make the hike more difficult. There is a greater amount of gullies and boulders at the more southern base of the mountain.) Scramble up through bushes and boulders to the center of the ravine where a rocky wash pro-vides easier traveling. Follow the ravine to a false summit. From here, look ESE to see the true summit. Bushwhack and scramble over rocky, densely vegetated terrain to reach the gentle, west-facing slope that leads to the summit.

Note: From the summit, it appears that there is an easier, more straight-forward route through Conejo Well and up the north side of Eagle Peak. This is an illusion to say the least. The northern route does provide an easier

140

approach to the base. In addition, the scramble from the false summit to the real summit is avoided. However, the actual climb up the mountain is more difficult, route finding is more difficult, and the route is three miles longer one-way.

6. MOORTEN'S MILL / LITTLE CHILCOOT PASS

Type: x-country, day
Mileage: 1.3 miles (round-trip)
Time: 1 hour
Difficulty: easy
Elevation Extremes: 2820' - 3010'   **Difference:** 190'
Starting and Ending Point: Cottonwood Spring Parking (3010')
Topo Map: Cottonwood Spring 7.5'   **Appendix D Map:** # 11

Summary: A hike over an old teamster's route leads to the site of a 5-stamp mill. "Cactus" Slim Moorten built the mill in the 1930's to process ore from his nearby claims.

The remains at the mill, which include a foundation, an old vehicle, and rusted tanks, are meager. However, it's the route to the site, not the mill site itself, that makes this hike interesting. The route travels through a wash rich with Colorado Desert flora. Mesquite, palo verdes, willows, and yuccas dominate the vegetation.

The teamster's route was the wagon road used to reach Cottonwood Spring in the early 1900's. The majority of the road has vanished; however, you can still see a short section of the road known as Little Chilcoot Pass. Little Chilcoot Pass was built to bypass a low cliff in the wash.

Route: Follow the wash south from Cottonwood Spring. Travel over Little Chilcoot Pass, 1/4 mile from Cottonwood Spring , and continue down the wash to Moorten's Mill. The mill site is on the right side of the wash below a hill. Watch for the wooden post with an arrow that points to the site.

7. MASTODON PEAK LOOP

Type: trail, day
Mileage: 2.5 mile loop
Time: 2 hours
Difficulty: moderate, moderate scrambling up the peak
Elevation Extremes: 2990' - 3360'   **Difference:** 370'
Starting and Ending Point: Cottonwood Spring Parking (3010')
Topo Maps: Cottonwood Spring 7.5'   **Appendix D Map:** # 11

Summary: The Mastodon loop travels past two sites that were busy during the mining days. Traveling counter-clockwise from Cottonwood Spring, the trail passes Mastodon Mine and then Winona Mill site. Mastodon Mine was a gold mine that operated between 1919 and 1932. The open mine shafts can still be seen today. (Do not enter mine shafts. They are unstable and dangerous.)

Mastodon Peak (3440') lies just above the mine. Invite your imagination to mimic that of the early prospectors who named this peak. They imagined the rock formation, which creates the peak, to be a likeness of a prehistoric elephant head. A short spur-trail leads to the summit of the peak. The impressive views from the peak include the Cottonwood area, Eagle Peak, Monument Mountain, Mt. San Jacinto, Shavers Valley, and the Salton Sea. Look for the marked trail junction around mile 0.9 on the loop. From the junction, a rough, unmaintained trail leads 0.1 miles to the summit. Although the climb is not difficult, it is narrow, exposed, and involves some rock scrambling.

About a mile past Mastodon Mine lies Winona Mill. Winona was the site of a small village and mill that was active in the 1920's. Gold ore from the Mastodon Mine and other nearby mining claims was processed at this mill. The foundations of the mill buildings still dot the hillside. Cottonwoods and exotic trees and shrubs, which were planted by the millhands, flourish in a wash at the base of the hill. The large trees provide habitat for birds and wildlife and shade for passing hikers. The loop continues from Winona back to the Cottonwood Spring parking lot.

8. LOST PALMS OASIS

Type: trail, day/overnight (note day use area on map)
Mileage: 7.5 miles (round-trip)
Time: 4 - 6 hours
Difficulty: moderate (to the oasis overlook)
Elevation Extremes: 2990' - 3450'   **Difference:** 460'
Starting and Ending Point: Cottonwood Spring Parking (3010')
Topo Maps: Cottonwood Spring 7.5'   **Appendix D Map:** # 11

Summary: Lost Palms Oasis is one of the largest palm oases in the park. It rivals Munsen Canyon in the number of palms in one canyon (more than

100 palms in each canyon). However, Lost Palms Oasis has a larger concentration of palms in a single area.

The trail to the oasis overlook travels through sandy washes and rolling hills. The overlook is the end of the "moderate" portion of the hike. A steep, rugged, strenuous trail leads down to the oasis and canyon bottom. Beneath

*Towering palms and canyon walls dwarf a hiker
at Lost Palms Oasis.*

the towering fan palms, water trickles down through the sandy wash then disappears in a rocky boulder canyon below. The echoing of the canyon wren's song and the rustling of the palms add to the beauty of this remote area. In the upper end of the oasis, there is a rugged, boulder-strewn side canyon. A hike up that canyon leads to Dike Springs and more palm stands.

Watch for animal tracks and droppings along the trail and in the canyon bottom. The combination of the water, rugged terrain, and remoteness of the area makes Lost Palms Oasis ideal habitat for the elusive bighorn sheep. Although overnight camping is not permitted at the oasis, camping is allowed in the rolling hills before the overlook. (Note the day use area. Refer to Chapter 3, "Understanding Day Use Areas and Desert Bighorn Sheep.")

Victory Palms (2680'): Hiking one mile down the wash from Lost Palms Oasis leads to Victory Palms (only two palms). To reach these palms, either travel down through the canyon — which involves some difficult, though interesting, boulder scrambling — or follow an obscure trail along the south side of the canyon. To find the trail, follow the wash downhill 0.2 miles from Lost Palms Oasis. Look for a cairn; it marks the point where the trail leaves the right (southwest) side of the wash.

9. MUNSEN CANYON

Type: x-country, day/overnight (note day use area on map)
Mileage: 9 miles (round-trip) main oasis, 12 miles (round-trip) to uppermost oasis
Time: 7 - 10 hours, (9 - 12 hours)
Difficulty: strenuous, difficult
Elevation Extremes: 1880' - 3280' (4200')   **Difference:** 1400' (2320')
Starting and Ending Point: south boundary above Chiriaco Summit (1880')
Topo Maps: Hayfield 7.5', Cottonwood Spring 7.5'   **Appendix D Map:** # 11

Summary: This canyon has all the beauty and life of Lost Palms Canyon but on a larger scale. With over 110 palms, this canyon surpasses Lost Palms in the number of palms in one canyon. The palm stands, containing up to thirty-five trees, are spread out over a two-mile stretch. The two largest palm groves are located at Summit Springs and Munsen Oasis. Small stands of palms are interspersed between and beyond the two springs.

One of the most picturesque groves is in an upper side canyon. Large rock formations surround this remote grouping of fifteen palms. Traveling in this side canyon involves some of the most difficult boulder scrambling (difficult+) of the entire hike.

The remote location and rugged terrain of Munsen Canyon create a haven for wildlife. The seclusive bighorn sheep inhabit the upper reaches of the canyon. Because it is bighorn habitat, the canyon is included within a day use area. (Refer to Chapter 3, "Understanding Day Use Areas and Desert Bighorn Sheep.") Camping is allowed either near the beginning of the hike or in the upper side canyon past the last palm stand. Reaching the latter location with a full backpack is very difficult and not recommended.

Route: A dirt road leads north from Chiriaco Summit to the park. The road is closed to vehicles about 1/4 mile north of the park boundary. Park at the road closure and hike up the road. The road soon disappears in a large sandy wash. Continue following the wash into a canyon. The canyon forks three miles from the boundary. Take the right fork. The left fork leads to Victory Palms. (See preceding hike, Lost Palms Oasis.)

At this point, travel changes from easy to difficult. Large boulders fill the canyon. Confidence in boulder scrambling is a necessity for continuing on this route. Summit Springs, the first of the two large palm groves, lies about 1/2 mile above this fork. Travel is easier between Summit Springs and Munsen Oasis (the largest palm grove in the canyon). However, there are still several boulder obstructions in this one mile section.

About 0.4 miles beyond Munsen Oasis, there is a side canyon. (A stand of fourteen palms grows at this junction.) This eastern side canyon leads to the picturesque grouping of fifteen palms noted in the hike summary. The side canyon eventually opens up to a rocky valley below Eagle Peak.

10. BAJADA TRAIL - (See Chapter 5, Hike # 13.)

Munsen Canyon leads to a rocky valley below Eagle Peak.

Chapter 16
WONDERLAND OF ROCKS

The Wonderland of Rocks is one of the most incredible areas within the park. Twelve square miles of massive monzogranite boulder piles create this jumbled maze. Within this stony wilderness, there are miniature Joshua tree forests tucked in verdant valleys; large willows surrounding ponds that attract a myriad of birds and other wildlife; sandy washes lined with giant flowering nolinas; intermittent streams flowing through a series of caves created by the haphazard lay of the boulders; and several small, clear pools of water that reflect the beautiful surroundings.

Hiking in the Wonderland is very difficult due to the rough terrain. Solo travel is discouraged except in the easier, established routes in the washes. A hiker who slips off a boulder while traveling down one of the many gullies could fall through a series of cracks and dropoffs created by the several layers of boulders. The maze-like nature of the Wonderland has proven to be a prison for those lost or injured and a difficult puzzle for those searching for the lost or injured. Proficient map and compass skills are essential for anyone venturing into the Wonderland.

The Wonderland can be accessed from either Park Boulevard or Indian Cove. Nearby campgrounds include Indian Cove, Hidden Valley, and Ryan. There are backcountry boards at Indian Cove and on Park Boulevard. Due to a resident population of bighorn sheep, the National Park Service has designated the Wonderland as a day use area. Camping is allowed along the outer edges of the Wonderland outside the restricted area. (Camping in the day use area is harmful to the bighorn. Refer to Chapter 3, "Understanding Day Use Areas And Desert Bighorn Sheep.") See map on page 148.

1. BIG BARKER DAM LOOP - (See Chapter 8, Hike # 1.)

Barker Dam creates a small, beautiful lake within the Wonderland.

2. WONDERLAND RANCH WASH

Type: x-country, day
Mileage: 2 miles (round-trip) to Astro Domes
Time: 1.5 hours
Difficulty: easy, easy scrambling
Elevation Extremes: relatively level
Starting and Ending Point: Wonderland Ranch Parking Area (4280')
Topo Map: Indian Cove 7.5'   **Appendix D Map:** # 7

Summary: Rock climbers frequently use this popular route to travel to the Astro Domes. The Astro Domes are a collection of giant, steep-faced boulders that provide climbers with some of the highest, most extreme climbs in the park. Some of these boulders tower over 300' above the wash. This hike provides an opportunity both to view some of these climbing extremists and to enjoy the natural beauty of the area. Several washes and canyons branch from this valley and lead to equally interesting, but confusing, maze-like areas.

Route: Follow the road-trail from the parking area to the ruins of a pink house (the former Wonderland Ranch). Head left (west) from the corner of the house and enter a wash fifty feet away. Travel northwest up the wash.

Watch for a thick growth of bushes and trees about 25 yards up the wash on the left side. Hidden behind the greenery is a site used first by early Indians and later by pioneers. Look under an overhanging boulder to find a cold storage compartment built by pioneers. On the nearby ledge, look for a bedrock mortar. A mortar is a smooth, deep hole in the rock in which early Native Americans ground seeds, acorns, or other raw foods.

Follow the wash and the intermittent parallel trail as they wind around bushes, oak trees, cacti, and boulders in the rocky corridor. The wash emerges in the valley below the Astro Domes.

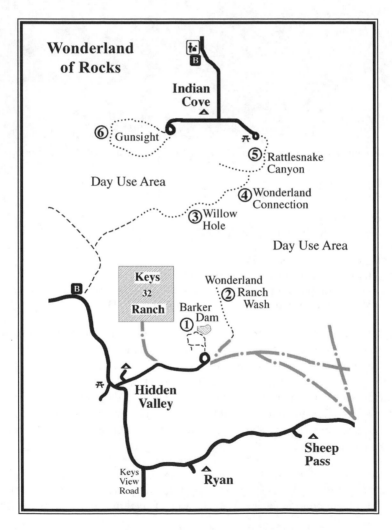

A hiker in Wonderland Ranch Wash looks for climbers on the South Astro Dome.

3. WILLOW HOLE

Type: trail/x-country, day
Mileage: 7 miles (round-trip)
Time: 4 hours
Difficulty: easy
Elevation Extremes: 4020' - 4140'   **Difference:** 120'
Starting and Ending Point: Boy Scout Trailhead (4040')
Topo Map: Indian Cove 7.5'   **Appendix D Map:** # 7

Summary: This is one of the easiest and most popular hiking routes into the Wonderland. The route travels through open desert then follows a wash that narrows as it winds through tall boulder piles. The wash widens just before Willow Hole where big willow trees and rocky walls surround large pools of water. (Water levels are dependent upon annual rainfall and time of year.)

Route: Follow the trail north 1.4 miles from the parking area to a fork in the trail. The left trail is the Boy Scout Trail. Take the right fork. Follow the trail until it disappears in the wash. Continue down the wash (about 0.7 miles) through a rocky corridor to Willow Hole.

149

4. WONDERLAND CONNECTION

Type: trail/x-country, day
Mileage: 5.5 miles (one-way)
Time: 6 hours
Difficulty: strenuous, difficult (+)
Elevation Extremes: 3017' - 4140'　　　**Difference:** 1123'
Starting Point: Boy Scout Trailhead (4040')
Ending Point: Indian Cove Picnic Area (3017')
Topo Map: Indian Cove 7.5'　　　**Appendix D Map:** # 7

Summary: This route passes through the heart of the Wonderland as it leads from Willow Hole to Indian Cove. The route follows a rocky wash where flowing water and small pools can be found throughout much of the year. It passes near boulder caves and through small valleys, including the valley of Oh-bay-yo-yo.

Since the early 1940's, local people have used the Oh-bay-yo-yo cave as a wilderness retreat. The cave is actually no more than a hollow under a boulder with walls constructed of sticks and rocks. However, the early hikers took pride (and still do) in their secluded fort. They kept a register in the cave. It was traditional for hikers to make a log entry with their name and the number of times they had completed the trek to Oh-bay-yo-yo.

The locals went to great pains to build the cave and to keep it stocked with supplies. One of the original builders made a log entry announcing that he had carried fifty pounds of flat rocks uphill from Indian Cove to build one of the cave walls. The fort was stocked with dishes, pans, food, matches, a lamp, and a Bible. The original register, as well as many of the supplies kept in the fort, has since disappeared. (Please leave what little remains at the retreat.)

This hike through the Wonderland is beautiful and rewarding; however, the rugged terrain makes travel difficult and time-consuming. The route travels through a slick rock canyon where there are pools of water and giant rock slabs to crawl around, over, or under. This hike should only be attempted by those proficient in boulder scrambling. Don't be deceived by the fact that this hike is all downhill — allow plenty of time to complete the trip. (Camping is not allowed in the Wonderland. Refer to Chapter 3, "Understanding Day Use Areas and Desert Bighorn Sheep.")

Route: Hike to Willow Hole (see preceding hike) then exit the wash on the right side. Travel through the south half of the willow grove to reach a small cove at the rear of the grove. Travel 50' along a well-beaten path on the right side of the cove. This path leads to the top of a low ridge. From the top of the ridge, head E 100 yards through a relatively flat, open area to reach a gap between two rock piles. Climb down through the gap and drop into a narrow boulder-strewn wash. Follow the course of the wash through the rocks.

Continue following the wash as it makes a sharp bend to the left* and then to the right. The wash becomes boulder-clogged; further travel involves difficult rock scrambling. (* Use caution at this turn. There is a tendency to miss the turn, exit the wash, and travel *up* into an open area. After leaving the low ridge above Willow Hole, all travel should be *downhill.)*

About 0.7 miles from Willow Hole, the wash intersects a north/south wash. Just before this intersection, there is an open, flat area. From here a trail leads to the left (north) to Oh-bay-yo-yo.

Continue traveling north in the north/south wash to reach the upper sections of Rattlesnake Canyon. (The last section of the north/south wash is steep and travel is very difficult.) Head NE down Rattlesnake Canyon. See Chapter 12, Hike # 5, for the description of the remaining hike to Indian Cove.

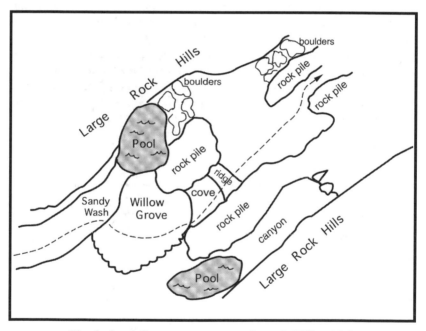

Wonderland Connection: route through Willow Hole

5. RATTLESNAKE CANYON - (See Chapter 12, Hike # 5.)

6. GUN SIGHT LOOP - (See Chapter 12, Hike # 3.)

Chapter 17
COXCOMB MOUNTAINS

The Coxcomb Mountain Range is a wilderness of remote, highly distinctive, rugged peaks. The area is a sanctuary for desert bighorn sheep. The sheep roam at ease, but in limited numbers, through this isolated maze of mountains. (Watch for signs of sheep but avoid disturbing this diminishing species. Refer to Chapter 3, "Understanding Day Use Areas and Desert Bighorn Sheep.") The sandy washes that wind through these mountains aid travel and route-finding; however, proficient map and compass skills are still essential for exploring this towering jumble of rocks.

Access to the Coxcombs is from Highway 177 along the east boundary of the park or from Highway 62 along the north boundary (39 miles east of Twentynine Palms). There are no campgrounds or towns for miles in any direction. Since there are no backcountry boards, those interested in overnight hikes should inquire and register at the Oasis Visitor Center in Twentynine Palms.

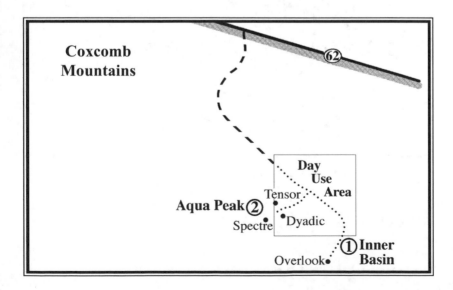

1. INNER BASIN OVERLOOK

Type: x-country, day/overnight (note day use area on map)
Mileage: 17 miles (round-trip)
Time: 10 hours
Difficulty: moderately strenuous, moderately difficult
Elevation Extremes: 1700' - 3050'   **Difference:** 1350'
Starting and Ending Point: Coxcomb Parking Area (1700')
Topo Map: Cadiz Valley SW 7.5, Cadiz Valley SE 7.5'   **Appendix D Map:** # 1

Summary: This route provides the easiest access into the most rugged portion of the Coxcombs. The route travels through washes and along rocky ridges to a basin within the mountains. A trip to the edge of this basin leads to a high overlook of Pinto Basin. Most of the hike to the Inner Basin travels through a day use area. Camping is permitted near the first four miles of the route and in the southern end of the basin.

Several side trips can be made from the Inner Basin. At the southern end of the basin, a wash heads west up into the rocky mountains. This same wash leads southeast down through steep-walled canyons. Yet another hike leads down the overlook to Pinto Basin, around the base of the mountains, and back to the parking area.

Route: From the parking area, walk about 4.5 miles south on a closed road and wash. The wash leads into a boulder canyon. Scramble southeast up through the canyon and wash to a pass. Cross the pass, then drop into another wash that leads southeast. Follow this wash down to a wash junction and continue southeast. (The main wash leads down to the NNE.) Travel is now uphill in the wash. This wash leads to the Inner Basin. To reach the overlook, follow the wash out into the basin where it curves SSW then W. When the wash starts to curve W, leave the wash and continue traveling SSW to the edge of the basin and the overlook.

2. AQUA PEAK (TENSOR, SPECTRE, DYADIC) 4416'

Type: x-country, day/overnight (note day use area on map)
Mileage: 15 miles (round-trip)
Time: 10 - 12 hours
Difficulty: strenuous, difficult (+)
Elevation Extremes: 1700' - 4416'(+)   **Difference:** 2716'
Starting and Ending Point: Coxcomb Parking Area (1700')
Topo Map: Cadiz Valley 15' or Cadiz Valley SW 7.5'   **Appendix D Map:** # 1

Summary: Aqua Peak is a collective name for three high peaks located in close proximity. These peaks are the highest in the Coxcomb Mountains. They are the most difficult peaks to climb of all the peaks described in this

A hiker on Spectre Peak is rewarded with a bird's-eye view of the Coxcomb Mountains.

guide. Climbers in the 1940's named these peaks Tensor, Spectre, and Dyadic. Since then, the USGS has installed a benchmark on Tensor, the lowest of the three peaks. The benchmark names the peak "Aqua" and records the elevation as 4416'.

The summit of Tensor is the easiest to reach of the three peaks. Dyadic's summit is the most difficult to attain and is seemingly the highest of the three summits. Reaching the top of Dyadic requires short sections of technical climbing (5.1-5.4) near the summit. Attaining the summits of Tensor and Spectre involves difficult boulder scrambling but not technical climbing. All three peaks are reached from a plateau that lies at an elevation of 4080'. The longest and most strenuous part of the hike is the ascent up the rocky gully that leads to this plateau. All three peaks have summit registers.

Route: From the parking area, walk about 4.5 miles south on a closed road and wash. The wash leads into a boulder canyon. Climb southeast up the rocky wash to a pass. Descend to a sandy wash on the other side of the pass. About 1/4 mile from the pass, the wash makes a sharp bend to the left and begins to wind through a narrow canyon. Do not enter the canyon. Leave the wash before the sharp bend and continue heading SE over a ridge. Travel west up the major wash that lies at the bottom of this ridge.

Continue one mile up this steep, rocky wash/gully until it levels out on a plateau. Locate the three peaks from this plateau. Tensor is the rounded peak to the NNE; Spectre is the pointed peak to the SSW; Dyadic lies to the SSE. Dyadic is not readily visible from the plateau but can easily be seen from the slopes of Spectre and Tensor. Dyadic is the rock peak with a tall stake planted on the summit. Choose your peak and scramble the remaining distance.

Chapter 18
CASTLES AND ARCHES
THE ADVENTURE OF HIKING IN
JOSHUA TREE NATIONAL PARK

This final chapter presents a challenge — the challenge to embark on an adventure. The adventure might be the search for a castle, a mysterious place within the park that has eluded hikers for many years. Or it might be the challenge to locate the park's largest known arch, only recently discovered. Or it could be a self-proclaimed adventure. This chapter is not meant to guide the hiker to another special place. Its purpose is to establish an awareness of the unlimited hiking adventures that exist within Joshua Tree National Park. Hiking with a guide book is just the beginning.

There are not many people who know about the prospector's castle that lies in a rugged and isolated section of Joshua Tree National Park. Much of the history surrounding the castle is a mystery. A single man occupied this castle sometime around 1940. It is not known from where this man came or to where he went. The fact that he lived at the site around 1940 is surmised from a collection of dated magazines that were found in a cave near the castle.

The prospector's self-proclaimed castle is by no means elaborate. In fact, it's not a castle by dictionary definition. In actuality, it is only a small single-room house built under a giant boulder. The prospector used mortar and rocks from the desert to fill in the gaps between the boulder walls. He finished the house with steps, a hinged door, screen windows, and a chimney. Inside the house, there were all the comforts of home — a bed, chair, and a table.

The prospector's castle may not be as glamorous as a real castle, but it is unique. It is an example of how someone can adapt to a harsh desert environment and build a house from raw natural resources. Anyone with money can build a castle, but only a person with determination and a love for the desert can take the resources at hand and make the desert into a pleasing, satisfying home.

Note to castle hikers: Please don't disturb the castle. It is in excellent condition. (Do not remove "historical litter", for example tin cans, magazines.) Allow other hikers to experience this unique, undisturbed site.

The Castle

Another adventure may be the quest to find Garrett's Arch. The arch is deep in the heart of the Wonderland of Rocks and high up in a large rock formation. Blue sky colors the opening beneath the arch. This creates the appearance of a large eye staring from the head of a giant rock monster. From the valley floor, the arch appears dwarfed by the large rock faces that flank both sides of the tunnel opening. However, the vegetation surround-

157

ing the arch puts the size of the arch back in perspective. A mature oak tree growing in the opening under the arch only fills up about 1/3 of the opening.

The hike to the arch involves easy traveling. And the arch itself is readily visible from the valley floor. However, the trick to reaching the arch is locating the correct valley. The Wonderland consists of a maze of valleys nestled between large rock formations.

This book has described a select sampling of some of the most interesting and most notable areas within the of the park. However, this guide is not meant to provide descriptions and directions to every place of interest within the park. To do so would take away the adventure and mystery surrounding that which is unknown about this desert wilderness. To be able to hike through a remote area and not know exactly what will be found is exciting. To discover something new while hiking in that area is rewarding. To search for the rumored existence of a special place is an adventure.

The quest to find the prospector's castle or Garrett's Arch is an exciting adventure, but an adventure can be found on any hike within the park. Everyone who hikes in the desert, either on a described guidebook route or on a self-chosen route, will find something that is new and exciting to them. The desert wilderness holds many secrets and natural wonders that are waiting to be explored or discovered by those who travel **On Foot in Joshua Tree National Park.**

Appendix A
Landmark Descriptions
and Directions

Barker Dam Parking Area — Follow the paved road that leads northeast past the entrance to Hidden Valley Campground. Continue to a large parking lot at the end of the paved road.

Belle Campground — on Pinto Basin Road; 1.3 miles south of Pinto Wye; 28 miles north of Cottonwood Visitor Center

Berdoo Canyon Road — 4x4 road. Follow the Geology Tour Road 7.7 miles south of Park Boulevard to a point where the road forks. The right fork is the continuation of GTR. The left fork is the Berdoo Canyon Road.

Black Rock — Follow Joshua Lane south off Highway 62 in Yucca Valley. Follow the signs to reach the campground, ranger station, and visitor center.

Black Rock Trailhead — marked by large trailboard on the left (east) side of the Black Rock Campground entrance road, just inside the boundary

Borrow Pit Parking Area — small parking area located on the north side of a bend in Park Boulevard; 1.8 miles east of the West Entrance Station (A large parking lot, in the same general location, is forthcoming for this trailhead.)

Boy Scout Trailhead — located at a bend in Park Boulevard; 2.3 miles west of Hidden Valley Picnic Area; 6.5 miles from the West Entrance

Cap Rock Parking Area — first parking area on the left (east) side of Keys View Road; 0.2 miles south of Park Boulevard junction

Canyon Road — leads south from Highway 62 to the 49 Palms parking area; 4 miles west of Adobe Road in 29 Palms; 1.75 miles east of Indian Cove Road

Chiriaco Summit — on Interstate 10; 4.5 miles east of Pinto Basin Road

Coachella Valley — low desert valley located south of the park; location of desert communities such as Palm Springs, Indio, Palm Desert, etc.

Cottonwood Campground — located off of the Cottonwood Spring Road, which starts just south of the Cottonwood Visitor Center

Cottonwood Spring Parking — located at the end of the paved spur road that begins just south of Cottonwood Visitor Center; location of the Cottonwood Backcountry Board

Cottonwood Visitor Center — near the south entrance to the park on Pinto Basin Road; 7 miles north of Interstate 10

Covington Flats Backcountry Board — Take La Contenta Road south off Hwy 62, east of Yucca Valley. Cross Yucca Trail/Alta Loma and continue on a dirt road. Follow the dirt road to a junction on the left side (2.8 miles from Hwy 62). Watch for the "Covington Flats" sign. Turn left and continue 1.7 miles to the park boundary. Continue an additional 4.2 miles past the boundary to a junction. Turn right. Continue to another junction and turn left. Follow the road to the end.

Covington Flats Picnic Area — Take La Contenta Road south off Hwy 62, east of Yucca Valley. Cross Yucca Trail/Alta Loma and continue on a dirt road. Follow the dirt road to a junction on the left side (2.8 miles from Hwy 62). Watch for the "Covington Flats" sign. Turn left and continue 1.7 miles to the park boundary. Continue an additional 4.2 miles past the boundary to a junction. Continue straight past the junction to the end of the road.

Coxcomb Parking Area — From Utah Trail in 29 Palms, drive east on Hwy 62 approximately 39 miles. Watch for a closed dirt road/wash on the south side of the highway at a low point in the road. Park here along the roadside.

Desert Queen Ranch — Follow the dirt road that leads north from Echo Intersection. This is a pioneer ranch that is only accessible with park guided tours.

Dillon Road — road that parallels the southwest boundary of the park; accessible from Desert Hot Springs and Interstate 10

Echo Intersection — Follow the paved road that leads northeast past the entrance to Hidden Valley Campground. Continue 1/2 mile past the campground to the next road intersection.

Eureka Peak Parking — Take La Contenta Road south off Hwy 62, east of Yucca Valley. Cross Yucca Trail/Alta Loma and continue on a dirt road. Follow the dirt road to a junction on the left side (2.8 miles from Hwy 62). Watch for the "Covington Flats" sign. Turn left and continue 1.7 miles to the park boundary. Continue an additional 4.2 miles past the boundary to a junction. Turn right. Continue to another junction and turn right. Follow the road to the end.

Fried Liver Wash, Pinto Basin Road — mile wide wash that crosses Pinto Basin Road near mile 13

Geology Tour Road (GTR) — heads south off Park Boulevard; 5 miles west of Pinto Wye; 2.4 miles east of Sheep Pass

Geology Tour Backcountry Board — on left side of GTR; 1.4 miles south of Park Boulevard

Hidden Valley Campground — on a side road that leads northeast off of Park Boulevard; 4.3 miles west of Sheep Pass; 9 miles east of the West Entrance

Hidden Valley Picnic Area — on the south side of Park Boulevard; 8.8 miles east of the West Entrance Station; 4.4 miles west of Sheep Pass

Highway 62 — Twentynine Palms Highway; runs east/west along the north boundary of the park; access from Interstate 10 near Palm Springs

Indian Cove Road — leads south off Hwy 62; 5.7 miles west of Adobe Road in 29 Palms; 9 miles east of Park Boulevard in Joshua Tree; leads to a ranger station, picnic area, and campground

Indian Cove Backcountry Board — on the right (west) side of Indian Cove Road; 0.4 miles south of the Indian Cove Ranger Station

Indian Cove Picnic Area — located at the far left (east) end of Indian Cove Campground

Interstate 10 — Interstate Highway that runs east/west; one mile south of the park's South Entrance

Joshua Tree — small town on the north boundary of the park near the West Entrance; access by Highway 62

Jumbo Rocks Campground — on Park Boulevard; 3.4 miles west of Pinto Wye; 4 miles east of Sheep Pass

Juniper Flats Backcountry Board — on right (west) side of Keys View Road; one mile south of Park Boulevard junction

Keys View — end of Keys View Road

Keys View Road — heads south off Park Boulevard; about 3 miles west of Sheep Pass; 10.5 miles east of West Entrance

Live Oak Picnic Area — on the south side of Park Boulevard; 2 miles west of Pinto Wye; 5.3 miles east of Sheep Pass

Lost Horse Mine Parking — Follow Keys View Road south 2.4 miles from Park Boulevard. Turn left (east) onto dirt road and follow it to the end.

Lost Horse Valley — one of the two large valleys in the northwest part of the park; access by Park Boulevard and Keys View Road

Lucky Boy Junction — A dirt road leads north off Park Boulevard, opposite the Geology Tour Road. Travel north about one mile to a dirt pullout on the right (east).

Mt. San Gorgonio — prominent peak (11,499') located west of park

Mt. San Jacinto — prominent peak (10,804') located south of park

North Entrance — end of Utah Trail; 4 miles south of Hwy 62

North Entrance Backcountry Board — located on the east side of Park Blvd; 0.5 miles inside the North Entrance at the end of a short dirt road

North Entrance Exhibit — located 0.5 miles south of the North Entrance on the west side of the road

Oasis Visitor Center — main visitor center located at park headquarters on

Utah Trail in 29 Palms, 0.5 miles south of Hwy 62

O'Dell Parking Area — Follow Queen Valley Road, a dirt road that leads northwest from Park Boulevard; 1.6 miles east of Sheep Pass; 2.4 miles west of Jumbo Rocks Campground. Take a right at the dirt road fork. Follow the road north to the end.

Onaga Trail — a dirt road leading east off Park Boulevard, 1.8 miles south of Highway 62 in Joshua Tree. Leads to a primitive day use area administered by the town of Joshua Tree.

Park Boulevard — main east/west road between the North Entrance and West Entrance

Pine City Backcountry Board — A dirt road heads north off Park Boulevard, opposite the Geology Tour Road. Follow it north to the end (1.2 miles).

Pinkham Canyon Jeep-Trail — heads west off Pinto Basin Road near the Cottonwood Visitor Center; rough four-wheel drive dirt road

Pinto Basin Road — main north/south road between Pinto Wye and I-10

Pinto Wye — junction of Park Boulevard and Pinto Basin Road; 4.6 miles south of the North Entrance; 35.7 miles north of the South Entrance and 20.6 miles east of the West Entrance

Pinyon Well Parking Area — southwest corner of the one-way loop on Geology Tour Road; 9.5 miles from Park Boulevard; stop #15 GTR

Pleasant Valley Backcountry Board — at the end of the first leg of the Geology Tour Road's one-way loop; 6.8 miles from Park Boulevard

Porcupine Wash Backcountry Board — west side of Pinto Basin Road; 21.3 miles south of Pinto Wye; 8.4 miles north of Cottonwood Visitor Center

Quail Springs Picnic Area — south side of Park Boulevard; 3 miles west of Hidden Valley Campground; 5.9 miles east of the West Entrance. A road-trail leaves from the southwest corner of the back parking lot.

Radio Tower Road — From Hwy 62, travel south on Acoma Trail. Drive a little more then two miles to a dirt road intersection Turn west (right) and drive about 0.4 miles to another junction. Turn left (south). The road forks within 100 yards. Take the left fork. Drive one mile to the Radio Tower Road Junction. The tower is visible at this junction. Turn right and travel 1/2 mile southwest up Radio Tower Road. Just below the tower, there is a sharp road bend with a rock/cement drainage ditch on the left side. At this point, there is a gully on the left side of the road. This gully leads down to Long Canyon. (Although these dirt roads may be rough, four-wheel drive is usually not necessary.)

Ryan Campground — on Park Boulevard; 2.2 miles west of Sheep Pass; 11 miles east of the West Entrance

Ryan Mountain Parking Area — south side of Park Boulevard; 0.7 miles west of Sheep Pass; about 12.5 miles east of the West Entrance

Ryan Ranch Parking Area — south side of Park Boulevard; just east of the Ryan Campground entrance road.

Salton Sea — large lake (35 miles x 15 miles), located south of park

Santa Rosa Mtns. — distant mountain range located south of the park and south of Coachella Valley

Sheep Pass — a group campground and road pass on Park Boulevard; 12 miles from the North Entrance; 13.2 miles from the West Entrance

South Park Parking Area — Follow the dirt road that leads west immediately before the entrance to Black Rock Campground. Travel to the parking lot at the end of the road.

Split Rock Picnic Area — on the north side of Park Boulevard; 2 miles west of Pinto Wye; 6 miles east of Sheep Pass

Squaw Tank — stop # 9 on Geology Tour Road; 5.3 miles from Park Boulevard junction

Stop # 7 — on Geology Tour Road; 4.6 miles south of Park Boulevard junction

Stop # 14 — on Geology Tour Road; 9.5 miles from Park Boulevard junction

Turkey Flats Backcountry Board — on east side of Pinto Basin Road; 16.2 miles south of Pinto Wye; 13.5 miles north of Cottonwood Visitor Center

Twentynine Palms — small city on the north boundary of the park near the North Entrance; access by Highway 62

Twin Tanks Backcountry Board — on west side of Pinto Basin Road; 2.2 miles south of Pinto Wye; 27.5 miles north of Cottonwood Visitor Center

Two Knolls — two small, isolated hills located just south of Pinto Basin Road; 0.42 miles northwest of Cholla Cactus Garden

Utah Trail — the entrance road to the park; leads south off Hwy 62 at the east end of Twentynine Palms; passes Park Headquarters

West Entrance — location of fee collection station, water, and restrooms at the park's west boundary on Park Boulevard; 5 miles south of Hwy 62 in the town of Joshua Tree

West Entrance Wash — 1.2 miles east of the West Entrance. There's a small pullout on the north side of the road near the wash.

White Tank Campground — on Pinto Basin Road; 2.7 miles south of Pinto Wye; 27 miles north of Cottonwood Visitor Center

Wonderland of Rocks — geological feature in north center of park

Wonderland Ranch Parking — Turn north off Park Boulevard on the paved road that leads northeast past the entrance to Hidden Valley Campground. Travel about 1.5 miles to Queen Valley Dirt Road. Turn right onto the dirt road and travel about 0.15 miles. Take the first left and follow the short road to the end.

Yucca Valley — small town on the northwest boundary of the park

Appendix B
GLOSSARY
Of Common Terms and Abbreviations

alluvial fan — large sloping areas at the base of mountains. The slopes were formed by deposited sediments that were carried out of the mountains with rainwater run-off.

arrastra — drag stone mill used for crushing ore

b/c — backcountry board; place to register for overnight hikes

bedrock mortar — a hole in a rock in which American Indians ground seeds

cairn — pile of rocks or stones used as a trail marker or summit marker

Class III climbing — difficult scrambling over rocks; hands, as well as feet, might be used to ascend. A rope is sometimes desired.

Class IV climbing — climbing rocks with the use of hands and feet. A rope is used for inexperienced climbers.

desert varnish — dark mineral stain on rocks

GTR — Geology Tour Road; Chapter 9

inholding — private property within the park boundaries

petroglyph — rock carvings made by the early Native Americans. The carved symbols may have been a form of writing or perhaps just doodling.

QSPA — Quail Springs Picnic Area

slot canyon — narrow canyon between solid rock cliffs

tailings — crushed rocks that surround the entrance to many mine shafts.

tank — water-catch basin formed by a low dam spanning the width of a wash. Most of the tanks in the park are filled with sand.

wash — drainages and water paths that are dry except during rainstorms. Most desert washes are sandy.

x/c — x-country; traveling through the desert without the use of man-made travel aids

Appendix C
PEAK BAGGER'S GUIDE,
MILEAGE CHART,
EXTENDED TRIPS

Peak Bagger's Guide

Peak	Elevation	Elevation Gain	Hike Reference
Quail Mountain	5813'	2133'	Chap. 7, Hike # 5
		1473'	Chap. 10, Hike # 3
Queen Mountain	5687'	1207'	Chap. 8, Hike # 4
Inspiration Peak	5558'	408'	Chap. 10, Hike # 10
Eureka Peak	5518'	1538'	Chap. 13, Hike # 8
Ryan Mountain	5457'	977'	Chap. 7, Hike # 11
Little Berdoo Peak	5440'	2190'	Chap. 9, Hike # 8
Bernard Peak	5430'	2180'	Chap. 9, Hike # 8
Eagle Peak	5350'	2350'	Chap. 15, Hike # 5
Lost Horse Mtn.	5313'	713'	Chap. 10, Hike # 7
Warren Peak	5103'	1123'	Chap. 13, Hike # 4
Lone Tree Hill	5050'	230'	Chap. 13, Hike # 10
Negro Hill	4875'	439'	Chap. 8, Hike # 5
Monument Mtn.	4834'	2434'	Chap. 14, Hike # 11
		1594'	Chap. 15, Hike # 1
Lela Peak	4747'	1227'	Chap. 9, Hike # 3
Crown Prince	4581'	181'	Chap. 6, Hike # 10
Aqua Peak	4416'	1856'	Chap. 17, Hike # 2
South Park Peak	4395'	255'	Chap. 13, Hike # 2
Malapai Hill	4280'	520'	Chap. 9, Hike # 2
Pinto Mountain	3983'	2383'	Chap. 14, Hike # 9
Mary Peak	3820'	2064'	Chap. 14, Hike # 7
Joshua Mountain	3746'	1176'	Chap. 6, Hike # 2
Mastodon Peak	3440'	440'	Chap. 15, Hike # 7

Mileage Chart

All mileages are round-trip unless otherwise noted

(•) one way, requires vehicle shuttle   (!)   moderately difficult scrambling
(~) short section of easy to moderate   (!!) difficult scrambling/boulder hopping
     scrambling   (!!!) extra-difficult scrambling, climbing

Easy Hikes	Miles	Hours	Chapter #		Hike#
Botanical Walk	0.2	<1	5	Nature Trail	11
Bajada Trail	0.25	<1	5	Nature Trail	13
Cholla Cactus Garden	0.25	<1	5	Nature Trail	10
Keys View	0.25	<1	5	Nature Trail	6
Arch Rock	0.3	<1	5	Nature Trail	9
Cap Rock	0.4	<1	5	Nature Trail	7
Oasis of Mara	0.5	<1	5	Nature Trail	3
Indian Cove	0.6	<1	5	Nature Trail	2
Live Oak/Ivanpah	1	<1	6	Park Blvd East	6
Ryan Ranch Homestead	1	1	7	Park Blvd W.	10
Hidden Valley	1	1	5	Nature Trail	4
Moorten's Mill	1.3	1	15	Cottonwood	6
Barker Dam	1.3	1	5	Nature Trail	5
Cottonwood	1.4	1	5	Nature Trail	12
Wall Street Mill	1.5	1	8	Queen Valley	3
Oasis of Mara with extension	1.5	1	5	Nature Trail	3
Skull Rock	1.7	1	5	Nature Trail	8
Sand Dunes	2	1	14	Pinto Basin Rd	8
Wonderland Ranch Wash	2	1.5	16	Wonderland	2
Split Rock Loop	2.4	2	6	Park Blvd East	8
Lucky Boy Vista	2.5	2	8	Queen Valley	12
Pine City	3	2	8	Queen Valley	6
Big Barker Dam Loop	3	2	8	Queen Valley	1
Covington Crest	3	2-3	13	Black Rock	10
R&H: GTR - Pinto Rd (•)	4.5	2-3	11	CA R&H Tr.	4
Pleasant Valley Road-Trail	5	2-3	9	Geology Tour	4
Black Rock Canyon	5	2-3	13	Black Rock	3
R&H: Pinto Rd - N.Entrance (•)	7.3	3-4	11	CA R&H Tr.	5
Willow Hole	7	4	16	Wonderland	3
Quail Springs	7.8	4	7	Park Blvd West	3
Quail Springs Road/Wash (•)	8.5	5	7	Park Blvd West	3
Juniper Flats	9	4-6	10	Keys View	2
Eagle Mt. Road-Trail	11	5-6	15	Cottonwood	4
Fried Liver Wash (•)	14	7-9	9	Geology Tour	7

166

Moderate Hikes	Miles	Hours	Chapter #		Hike #
South Park Peak	0.7	1	13	Black Rock	2
Sneakeye Spring	1	1	12	Indian Cove	4
Silver Bell Mine	1	1	14	Pinto Basin Rd	4
Grand Tank (~)	1.25	1	14	Pinto Basin Rd	1
High View	1.3	1	5	Nature Trail	1
Desert Queen Mine	1.4	1	8	Queen Valley	8
Twin Tanks	2	1-2	14	Pinto Basin Rd	2
Mastodon Loop	2.5	2	15	Cottonwood	7
Crown Prince Lookout (~)	3	2	6	Park Blvd East	10
Lucky Loop (!)	3.2	2-3	8	Queen Valley	11
Eagle Cliff / Hills Mine	3.5	2-3	8	Queen Valley	10
Desert Queen Wash (•!)	3.5	2-3	8	Queen Valley	9
Covington Crest / Lone Tree	3.6	2-3	13	Black Rock	10
Short Loop	4	2-3	13	Black Rock	7
Lost Horse Mine	4	2-3	10	Keys View	6
Eldorado Mine	4	2-3	14	Pinto Basin Rd	4
Maze Loop	4.8	2-4	7	Park Blvd West	2
Pine City Canyon (•!!)	5.5	4	8	Queen Valley	7
Covington Loop	5.7	3-4	13	Black Rock	12
R&H: Keys Rd - GTR (•)	6.6	3-4	11	CA R&H Tr.	3
Black Rock - Covington (•)	7.6	3-5	11	CA R&H Tr.	1
Eldorado Mine (•)	7.5	4-5	9	Geology Tour	6
Lost Palms Oasis	7.5	4-6	15	Cottonwood	8
Boy Scout Trail (•)	8	4-5	7	Park Blvd West	7
Porcupine/Ruby Lee	8.5	5-6	14	Pinto Basin Rd	10
Smith Water Canyon (•!!)	8.5	5-7	13	Black Rock	13
Long Canyon / Chuckawalla	10	6	13	Black Rock	6
Johnny Lang Canyon (~)	10.5	6-7	7	Park Blvd West	6
Eldorado Mine	11	6-7	9	Geology Tour	6

Moderately Strenuous	Miles	Hours	Chapter #		Hike #
Pinto Wye Arrastra	1.25	1	6	Park Blvd East	5
Negro Hill	1.5	1.5	8	Queen Valley	5
Malapai Hill (!)	1.5	1-2	9	Geology Tour	2
Inspiration Peak (~)	1.4	1.5	10	Keys View	10
Pinto Wye Arrastra Loop (!!)	2	1.5	6	Park Blvd East	5
49 Palms Oasis	3	2-3	12	Indian Cove	6
Ryan Mountain	3	2-3	7	Park Blvd West	11
Contact Mine	3.4	2-3	6	Park Blvd East	3
Golden Bee Mine	3.5	2-3	14	Pinto Basin Rd	4
Lost Horse Mountain	4.5	3	10	Keys View	7

167

Moderately Strenuous (cont.)	**Miles**	**Hours**	**Chapter #**		**Hike #**
Eureka Peak (•)	5	3-4	13	Black Rock	8
Panorama Loop	5.6	4	13	Black Rock	5
Warren Peak (~)	6	3-4	13	Black Rock	4
Pushawalla Plateau	6.5	4-5	9	Geology Tour	9
North View / Window Rock	6.6	4-5	7	Park Blvd West	2
Burnt Hill Loop	7	4-5	13	Black Rock	9
Burro Loop	7.2	4-5	7	Park Blvd West	1
Johnny Lang Viewpoint	7.5	4-5	7	Park Blvd West	6
North View / Window Loop	7.6	5-6	7	Park Blvd West	2
Hexahedron Mine	8	5-6	9	Geology Tour	5
Lost Horse Loop	8.4	5-6	10	Keys View	8
R&H: Covington - Keys Rd (•)	11.3	5-7	11	CA R&H Tr.	2
Stubbe Spring Loop	12	6-8	10	Keys View	5
Blue Cut Loop	14.5	8-10	9	Geology Tour	10
Inner Basin (!)	17	10	17	Coxcomb	1

Strenuous Hikes	**Miles**	**Hours**	**Chapter #**		**Hike #**
Eagle Cliff Hills/Mine (!)	2.5	2-3	6	Park Blvd East	7
Joshua Mountain (!!)	2.6	2-3	6	Park Blvd East	2
Gun Sight Loop (!!!)	2.75	4	12	Indian Cove	3
Rattlesnake Canyon (!!)	3	3	12	Indian Cove	5
Queen Mountain (!)	4	3-4	8	Queen Valley	4
Lela Peak	5	3-4	9	Geology Tour	3
Wonderland Connection (•!!!)	5.5	6	16	Wonderland	4
Monument Mtn (!)	6	5-6	15	Cottonwood	1
Mary Peak	6.5	4-6	14	Pinto Basin Rd	7
Bernard/Berdoo Mts, Nard (!)	6.5	5-7	9	Geology Tour	8
49 Palms Canyon (!!!)	8	6-9	12	Indian Cove	7
Bernard/Berdoo Mts, Rt.#1 (!)	8.5	6-7	9	Geology Tour	8
Johnny Lang Mine	9	6-7	7	Park Blvd West	6
Pinto Mountain, S Wash (!!)	9	7-9	14	Pinto Basin Rd	9
Munsen Canyon (!!)	9	7-10	15	Cottonwood	9
Eagle Peak (!!)	10	8-10	15	Cottonwood	5
Bernard/Berdoo Mts, Rt.#2 (!)	11.5	6-8	9	Geology Tour	8
Munsen Canyon (!!)	12	9-12	15	Cottonwood	9
Quail Mountain	12	6-8	10	Keys View	3
Quail Mountain (!!)	12	7-9	7	Park Blvd West	5
Pinto Mountain, W. Wash (!!)	12	8-10	14	Pinto Basin Rd	9
Pinto Mountain, SE Wash (!)	13	8-10	14	Pinto Basin Rd	9
Aqua Peak (!!!)	15	10-12	17	Coxcombs	2
Monument Mtn (!)	20	12-14	14	Pinto Basin Rd	11

Extended Backpack Trips

The longest hike described in this guide is only 20 miles. However, the possibilities for planning extended backpack trips are limited only by the imagination. Days may be spent traveling through the park. Here are a few ideas for extended trips that involve combining several hikes described in the guide. (Numbers denote hike numbers, i.g., 5:4 is Chapter 5, Hike # 4.)

miles

Quail Mountain Loop   22.7

Hike from the Boy Scout Trailhead to Quail Springs Picnic Area via or adjacent to Park Boulevard. Climb up Quail Mountain via the north wash (7:5). Hike down Quail Mountain via the southeast ridge to Juniper Flats (10:3). Follow the California Riding & Hiking Trail west to Covington Flats (11:2). Hike down Smith Water Canyon and continue to Quail Springs Picnic Area (13:13). Travel back to the Boy Scout Trailhead via or adjacent to Park Boulevard.

Black Rock to Indian Cove   24.6

Hike the California Riding & Hiking Trail from Black Rock to Upper Covington Flats (11:1). Travel through Smith Water Canyon and continue to Quail Springs Picnic Area (13:13). Hike from Quail Springs Picnic Area to the Boy Scout Trailhead via or adjacent to Park Boulevard. Hike the Boy Scout Trail to Indian Cove (7:7).

California Riding & Hiking Trail from Black Rock to the   35.4
North Entrance (11:1-5)

Indian Cove Loop   38.7

Hike from Indian Cove to the Boy Scout Trailhead via the Boy Scout Trail (7:7). Hike the Quail Mountain Loop (described above). Travel back to Indian Cove via the Boy Scout Trail (7:7). (Note: The Wonderland Connection is not recommended for travel with a full backpack.)

Index of Hikes and Place Names

References and Suggested Readings

Bagley, Helen. *Sand in My Shoe*. Twentynine Palms, California: Homestead
   Press, 1978.
Greene, Linda W. *Historic Resource Study: A History of Land Use in Joshua Tree
   National Monument*. Denver, Colorado: U. S. Dept. of Interior, Denver
   Service Center, 1983.
Jaeger, Edmund C. *The California Deserts*. Stanford, California: Stanford
   University Press, 1965.
Joshua Tree Natural History Association. Leaflet series on flora, fauna, history,
   and geology of the park.
Knapp, Patty. *Getting to Know: Joshua Tree National Park*. Lebanon, ME:
   Children's Outdoor Library, 1995.
Miller, Ronald Dean. *Mines of the High Desert*, glendale, California; La Siesta
   Press, 1965.
Trimble, Stephen. *Joshua Tree: desert reflections*. Twentynine Palms, California:
   Joshua Tree Natural History Association, 1979.

Appendix D:
TOPOGRAPHICAL MAPS

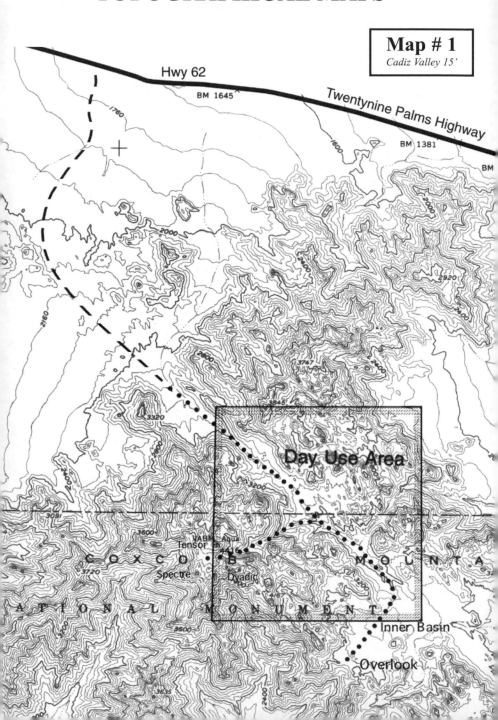

Map # 1
Cadiz Valley 15'

Hwy 62

BM 1645

Twentynine Palms Highway

BM 1381

BM

1760

1600

2000

2000

2920

2000

3747

1845

2900

3320

3091

3600

Aqua

Tensor

VABR

Dyadic

Spectre

C O X C O M B   M O U N T A

1720

3600

A T I O N A L   M O N U M E N T

Inner Basin

Overlook

Map # 2
Hexie Mountains 15'

Map # 3
Hexie Mountains 15'

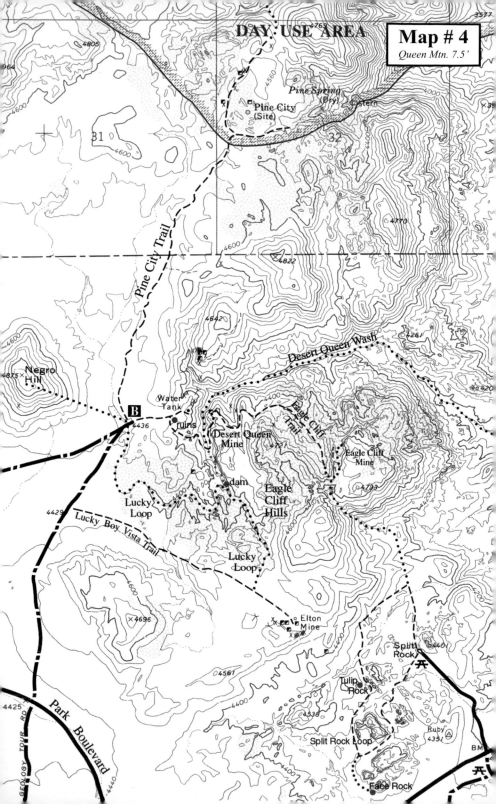

Map # 5

Joshua Tree 15'

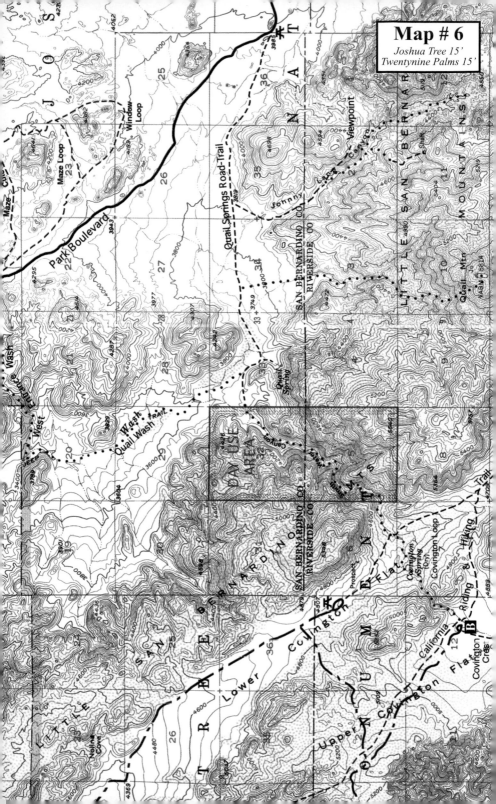

Map # 6
Joshua Tree 15'
Twentynine Palms 15'

Map # 7
Twentynine Palms 15'

Map # 8
Twentynine Palms 15'
Lost Horse Mtn. 15'

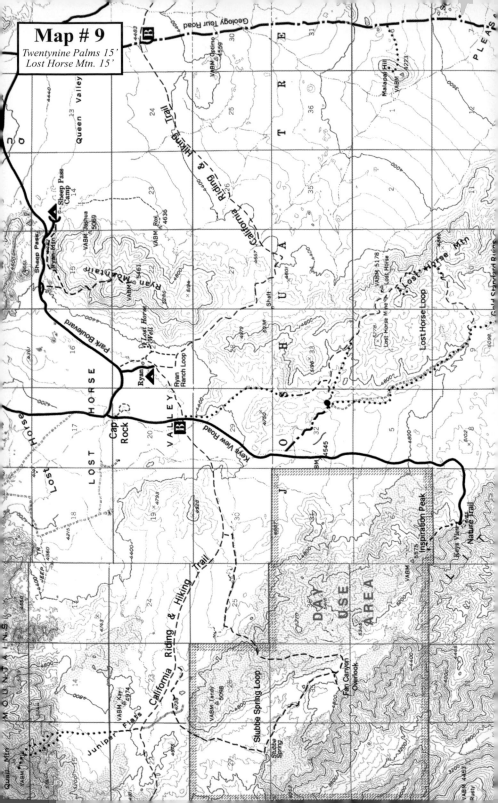

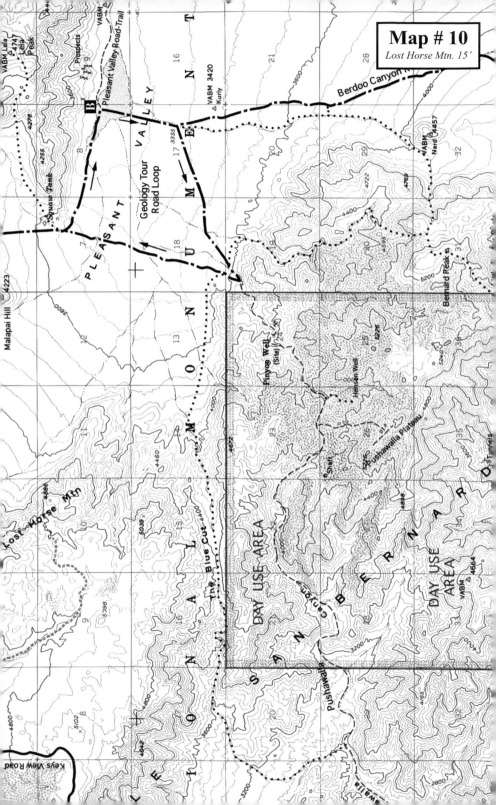

Map # 10

Lost Horse Mtn. 15'

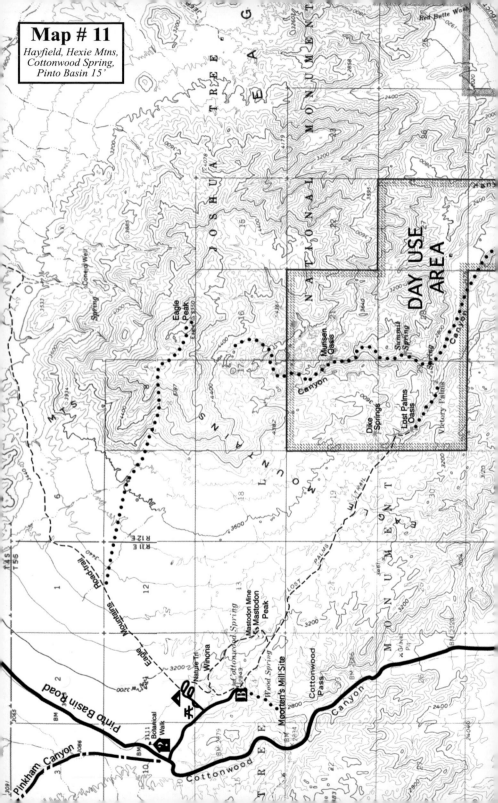

Map # 11
Hayfield, Hexie Mtns,
Cottonwood Spring,
Pinto Basin 15'